# MESSAGES
*from*
# MY HEART

*A Memoir of Healing & Transformation*

CAROLYN BOURNS

BALBOA.
PRESS

A DIVISION OF HAY HOUSE

Balboa Press books may be ordered through booksellers or by contacting:

Balboa Press
A Division of Hay House
1663 Liberty Drive
Bloomington, IN 47403
www.balboapress.com
1 (877) 407-4847

Because of the dynamic nature of the Internet, any web addresses or links contained in this book may have changed since publication and may no longer be valid. The views expressed in this work are solely those of the author and do not necessarily reflect the views of the publisher, and the publisher hereby disclaims any responsibility for them.

The author of this book does not dispense medical advice or prescribe the use of any technique as a form of treatment for physical, emotional, or medical problems without the advice of a physician, either directly or indirectly. The intent of the author is only to offer information of a general nature to help you in your quest for emotional and spiritual well-being. In the event you use any of the information in this book for yourself, which is your constitutional right, the author and the publisher assume no responsibility for your actions.

Any people depicted in stock imagery provided by Getty Images are models, and such images are being used for illustrative purposes only. Certain stock imagery © Getty Images.

Print information available on the last page.

ISBN: 978-1-9822-1647-4 (sc)
ISBN: 978-1-9822-1649-8 (hc)
ISBN: 978-1-9822-1648-1 (e)

Library of Congress Control Number: 2018913729

Balboa Press rev. date: 12/10/2018

# Dedication

Marion Roach tells us, "Memoir might best be described as a letter from the present and the past to the future." And so I dedicate this book to my grandchildren, Clayton, Jessica, and Thadeus; my great-grandchild, Hudson; and generations yet to come.

# Contents

*To realize one's destiny is a person's only obligation.*

—*Paulo Coelho, from* The Alchemist

# Foreword

*Messages from My Heart:*
*A Memoir of Healing and Transformation*
by Carolyn Bourns

If you've met Carolyn Bourns in person, you already know that she is an extraordinary presence. If you've yet to have that pleasure, know that you are about to "meet" her here in this beautifully written memoir. She tells her story with powerful openness, vulnerable authenticity, and abundant grace. I am confident that this is a meeting you will not soon forget.

I met Carolyn at the very first Story Alchemy Workshop I held in Southern California in August of 2015. As she participated in the seminar, I had no idea of all that she had endured and overcome in her life. Like many of us, Carolyn simply wanted to be well, to be free of pain and suffering— both medical and emotional, both relational and spiritual. But at the time of our first meeting, her bright smile and peaceful spirit betrayed none of that hard history. That was the past. Indeed, her remarkable story is what shaped her into the extraordinary person she is today.

I didn't realize it then, but that story workshop was another beginning, a new chapter in both of our journeys. This journey for Carolyn has culminated (for now) in the memoir you are holding in your hands and (for me) in the confirmation that story is always healing and transformative.

Before you embark on this journey with Carolyn, you should know that the *heart* of all great stories is the hero's transformation; however, the *power* of a great story is its ability to transform those of us who hear it. So prepare yourself.

Prepare to be transfixed and transformed, not only by Carolyn's resilience in adversity but by the inexplicable moments of Providence that cannot be dismissed as mere coincidence or even serendipity.

And then, once you have fully digested those miraculous, wondrous moments, prepare to be changed by the words that Spirit/Source/God audibly spoke to her at one of Carolyn's darkest moments. (In fact, a week doesn't go by that I don't remember and reflect on that one simple sentence. And I expect you will never forget it too.)

In her story, Carolyn has a message for you of healing and transformation, and I hope that you are open to receiving that gift. As you meet Carolyn in the pages that follow, you will quickly recognize that she radiates love from her whole being. I feel so blessed to be touched and even enveloped in that light.

After experiencing her story, I am confident that you will be touched and enveloped by her light too.
much JOY!

James R. Cichoracki, Ph.D.
February 2018 | Los Angeles
drjameskey.com

*One*

# IN THE BEGINNING

The older I get, the more vivid the events of my early childhood become as I contrast my life then with that of my grandchildren now. Travel with me for a moment back to 1944.

*I'm four years old, sitting up in what Mommy calls "the day bed." It's green and bumpy with buttons. Mostly now I spend all day here close to Mommy instead of in my bedroom down the stairs. You see, I have a romantic fever, and it can hurt my heart forever and ever, so I have to be very good and stay in bed. My big brother, Barney, makes me cry, so Mommy says he has to stay away from me because he's a big tease.*

*I like when it's night the best because I get to go into the living room and listen to stories. Sometimes there's a story on the radio like the Lone Ranger and Tonto, but the best is when Mommy reads us the Peter Pan story. We have to cover all the windows tight at night with blankets to black out the light. That's so the Japanese can't know where we are and come kill us.*

*In the day, I get so alone that sometimes I travel in my 'magination to see where Daddy is over the seas. Maybe we can help him doctor the soldiers fighting the bad Germans. You see, I'm Titi and my closest friend is Titi the Great. He teaches me how to fly and keeps me safe when we go far from my bed. I get hot and achy in the afternoon, so Mommy brings me aspirin. Sometimes Titi the Great eats my pill for me because I don't like the way it tastes icky-pulley in my mouth. It makes my tummy hurt until dinner. I don't tell Mommy though because she'll worry more that I won't get well.*

As a young child growing up during World War II, I felt confused, vulnerable, and broken. My lengthy convalescence from rheumatic fever led me to believe something was irreparably wrong with me. I would need to be taken care of and protected for the rest of my life. I craved connection, safety, and robust health. Even when I was eventually allowed to start school, I had to go lie down in the nurse's office while my classmates went out to play. I kept my feelings and resulting emotions buried deep inside so I could win favor with those I depended upon for survival in the uncertain world of my birth.

By adolescence, I had recovered; the only aftereffects of my long illness were a functional "murmur" and enlarged heart. I went on to do all that was expected of me growing up as a teen in the *Happy Days*–era of post-war America: bobby socks, saddle shoes, and pageboy haircut; high school student body president; off to college by eighteen to get my "Mrs."; married at nineteen; two darling sons by age twenty-two; and a college degree and teaching career by twenty-five. My husband, Lee, and I bought a home, a car, a truck-camper, and eventually a summer cabin in Idaho. We were living the American Dream promised us by our GI fathers.

And so, my dear grandchildren, in the following pages I wish to share a transitional portion of my life with you and generations to follow. I know that, at some point on your journey through this schoolhouse we call life, you will be challenged by unforeseen events and have to make decisions that will change your intended destination forever like it did mine. Blessings, my millennial grandchildren, on your journey.

*We have the universe to roam in in imagination.*
*It is our virtue to be infinitely varied.*
*The worst tyranny is uniformity.*

—*George William Russell*

*Part I*

# SPRING 1985 TO SPRING 1986

*Two*

# DENIAL

No matter how hard we strive, into each ordinary life come challenges. At age forty-five, I found myself in the waiting room of a doctor's office staring at a battered copy of *Sports Illustrated*—the only magazine left on the table beside me. The waiting room was filled to capacity with anxious and weary-looking patients, and I joined their ranks. I had been called for a return visit so my new physician could discuss the results of a diagnostic she had conducted to determine the activity of my heart for twenty-four hours. I had been having episodes of violent heart arrhythmias for a number of weeks. These palpitations could happen at any time, even awakening me in the middle of the night from a sound sleep. I would lie awake for minutes, and sometimes even hours, as the bed shook with the pounding inside my chest. Reluctantly, I finally took myself in to see my new doctor.

After about twenty minutes I was ushered into my physician's office to discuss her findings.

"Carolyn, the activity of your heart for the twenty-four hours you wore the monitor indicate that, even though you didn't feel the violent episodes that brought you into my office, your heart is going in and out of rhythm constantly. Are you using stimulants of any kind like excessive amounts of coffee or tea, over-the-counter or recreational drugs?"

I shook my head, no. Much like my mother, I had never done well with any kind of stimulant, so I followed her example and never got hooked.

My doctor continued her probing. "What are you doing for exercise? How much sleep are you getting? What is your diet like?"

Satisfied with all my responses, she paused, then looked up at me and asked the question that would forever change my life.

"Then, what *is* the stress in your life?"

I don't recall exactly how I responded. In the mid-eighties, the mind/body connection had not yet reached the mainstream, so it made no sense to me that your thoughts had anything to do with the functioning of your heart. My firm belief was that, when something went wrong in the body, there would be a drug or operation that would cure the problem. I had told this doctor about my childhood rheumatic heart disease. Surely that was the cause. I believe I responded to her last question by mentioning the stress of trying to meet the needs of thirty-four fifth graders. I declined her offer of drugs to relieve what she referred to as an anxiety disorder, wheeled out of her office, and hurried across the parking lot to my car with my head held high.

The next errand on my list for this rare leave day from my duties in the classroom was a visit to my twenty-five-year-old son, Michael, who was currently residing at a facility for drug and alcohol recovery. My hope was that this three-month program would result in lasting recovery. Four years earlier, his first program at a nearby psychiatric clinic had educated him on drug and alcohol addiction. Mike enjoyed sobriety for a few years, but suffered a severe relapse that had endangered his life.

Stress indeed! As I drove the considerable miles to Mike's location, I began to review the events of the past year. I had been through this kind of stress before, and my heart had withstood the anxiety that comes with having an addicted son. It couldn't be that. My non-steering hand rested on my beleaguered heart as I searched for answers. Was there anything else I might be stressed about?

My thoughts drifted back to the role alcohol had played in my life. When World War II was over and the soldiers returned from overseas, there was a lot of forgetting that went on. Alcohol became my parents' anesthesia of choice, so frequent alcohol consumption was familiar behavior to me.

When I met Lee, I didn't think much about his use of alcohol, which was constant. He could drink pretty much throughout the day with little effect. Was this a problem? He had always been highly functional, maintaining his dependency on alcohol to quiet the demons of a terrible childhood.

Later I learned that for some people, a high tolerance to the effects of spirits was the first of three stages in the disease of alcoholism. The second stage is increased consumption of intoxicants in an attempt on the part of the addictive-prone individual to get the same effect. During the third stage, the person's behavior becomes unpredictable and a serious danger to themselves and others. Once they started drinking for the day, it would be next to impossible to stop until unconscious. According to experts, there are only two ways out of stage-three alcoholism—abstinence or death.

Because of my oldest son's challenge with substance abuse, I joined a family support program for relatives and loved ones of alcoholics. Loren, the facilitator, was a no-nonsense individual with lots of experience in educating co-dependent enablers like me. Her working phrase for those of us in the group was: *You didn't cause it, you can't cure it, but you can contribute to it.* I wanted to know what I needed to do to change my behavior when dealing with my loved ones. I was determined to stop contributing to the problem.

When Mike completed his first program, he came away with an amazing amount of information about alcohol addiction. Both of my sons were concerned about their father's constant imbibing and kept imploring me to do something. I think the exact words were, "You're blowing it, Mom. Make him stop drinking." I had been telling myself for years that Lee was simply a maintenance drinker, not an alcoholic. After all, weren't alcoholics derelict in their duties, unable to keep a job, and constantly drunk? That was certainly not Lee—or was it?

Things had changed for the two of us in the past year. Lee was currently on disability leave from his teaching duties because of "high blood pressure," reportedly caused by stress in the classroom. He was home every day and going to the bar more frequently and for longer periods of time. There were even a few occasions when I had found him passed out in his car. He got home, but was unable to make it into the house. If I dared speak to him about how dangerous this was, he would get terribly upset with me and sink into a dark mood. Being the doormat in the family, my "peace at any cost" mentality caused me to bury my worry and fear and overcompensate for my husband's erratic behavior. Floating around at the frayed edges of my mind was the vision of him passing out behind the wheel of his car and maiming or even killing not just himself, but others. Everything we had worked so hard to build to keep us happy and secure was being terribly threatened, and I felt powerless to do anything about it.

The boys were more determined than I was to take action. Mike recommended we stage an intervention. When I asked what that was, he explained it as setting up a meeting with those close and important to the alcoholic and describing to him the effect his drinking was having on them. It was important that there be some sort of consequence or consequences if he did not stop drinking. The most effective consequence would be loss of employment if you could get the employer to help participate in the intervention. Loss of a tenured teaching position could be a strong incentive to sobriety.

So, with Michael and Richard urging me on, I made an appointment with Al Zamola, director of personnel at the district office. I dreaded that appointment. My job since I was young had been to cover for the alcoholics in my life—to keep our "looking good," looking good. I over-functioned and covered for their dysfunction. My part in this family dynamic was referred to as co-alcoholic or co-dependent. My loved ones could continue to abuse alcohol if their super-efficient daughter, wife, or mother would come to their rescue, cover for them, or bail them out when their drinking got them into trouble.

Lee and I had been teachers with the district for over twenty years, so I was on a first-name basis with the district personnel director. When I entered his office, Al gave me a warm greeting and a big hug, which made me feel a little better about the request I was about to make. When I asked if he would help with the intervention, Al looked very uncomfortable and initially I was afraid I had revealed my shameful family secret to someone who would be unwilling to betray "one of the guys." Instead he told me kindly that he had already had a one-on-one intervention with Lee in his office. Al then revealed that Lee was on leave from his duties in the classroom, not because of high blood pressure, but because parents had reported him numerous times for smelling of alcohol. He had been warned each time, and the situation had finally escalated to the point where Al had ordered Lee to use his accumulated sick leave and get help. Lee was told he would not be reinstated unless he entered a program and had verification of attending daily meetings and a minimum of one month of sobriety.

I remember how stunned I was at this deception and betrayal by the man I loved. Lee was eight years my senior, and I had always thought of him as the strong one who would take care of me and keep the boys safe. In my eyes, he had always been highly functional. There were so many good things about this man—inspirational and enthusiastic teacher and athletic coach, loving and attentive father, gentle and considerate lover. His mantra to me for years, recited especially in times of passion, had been, "I love you, I need you, I can't live without you." In fact lately he had been pressing me to agree to having a big celebration to renew our marriage vows to celebrate our twenty-fifth wedding anniversary.

After my visit to the district office, the boys and I decided that since loss of employment was not enough motivation to get their father to stop drinking, I would have to tell Lee I would leave him if he didn't stop drinking.

Nothing in my previous life had prepared me to confront the man I loved with this kind of ultimatum. What if he said no? I couldn't bear the thought of leaving my beautiful home, giving up my summers at our cabin in Idaho, and walking away from the life we had built together. All our friends were his colleagues and acquaintances. What would happen to my social contacts if I left him? I would be completely on my own. On the other hand, hadn't he declared how much he needed me, how he couldn't live without me? So, I made a calculated decision. My husband loves me so much, surely he will stop drinking to keep me.

During the intervention, Mike told his father about good Alcoholics Anonymous (AA) meetings he could attend in the area and how having a support group could help him get and stay sober. Lee promised us he would stop drinking, but he flat-out refused to have anything to do with AA or any other type of program. He was determined he could do this on his own.

And stop he did, but it was not easy. I remember the night he came to get me in the kitchen. Lee said he needed me to come into the hall bathroom right away. I followed him into the tiny space and he pointed up to the heater vent near the ceiling.

Lee took hold of my arm and whispered, "Can you hear them?"

"Hear who?"

"Listen to the voices coming from the vent. They're telling us what they're going to do to the United States."

I looked at him carefully. He appeared perfectly normal, although slightly agitated. What were the voices saying? I strained to hear, but no matter how hard I tried, I heard nothing but the sound of the fan.

"Just keep the light off," I said gently, "and the voices will stop."

"But it's important to hear what they're saying. I need to report it to the authorities."

It was at this point that I finally understood the toll years of heavy drinking could exact. My insanity was that I tried with all my might to hear those voices. I simply couldn't admit to myself how sick the man with whom I had shared so many happy years actually was. This dynamic is called denial, which is *not* a river in Egypt. It is something we all do when the truth is too painful to confront. Denial is a constant companion when you are struggling with alcoholism, whether you are the alcoholic or the co-dependent. We are powerless, however, to change anything in our life if we are unwilling to confront it and get brutally honest with ourselves.

Lee, bless his heart, detoxed cold turkey and stayed sober for a couple of months. Much of his agitation subsided, but he was very obviously depressed. Warm weather arrived, and I noticed he was spending an inordinate amount of time out in our tiny backyard watering. His mood lifted, and I began to get suspicious. Upon examining the storage shed out back, I found a stash of empty wine bottles. Shortly after this discovery, the news came that one of his longtime drinking buddies, who had moved to Utah the year before, was coming to visit. He and his wife wanted to take us to dinner.

It was at this point Lee sat me down and said, "I'm going to drink tonight, and you are not to say anything about it in front of Joe and Margaret."

The gauntlet had been thrown down, and I simply was not up to the challenge. I lacked the courage to say no—to pack up and leave.

Unfortunately, we continued our life very much as it had been before the intervention. Lee resumed his daily drinking. They say that alcoholism is a progressive disease. This means that even if you go for years without touching a drop of alcohol, if you start again you resume at exactly the same stage where you were when you stopped. Lee was no exception.

During that long drive to visit Mike, I felt like a dark curtain had finally lifted. Something had clicked inside me after this mind's eye review of recent events in my life, and I could see clearly that it was time to take action. As I turned into the long driveway leading up to the facility that housed my recovering son, I had a very clear knowing of what I needed to do to quiet and heal my pounding heart.

*There is a moment in our healing journey*
*when our denial crumbles,*
*we realize our experience and its continued effects on us*
*won't 'just go away.'*
*That's our breakthrough moment.*
*It's the sun coming out to warm the seeds of hope*
*so they can grow our personal garden of empowerment.*

—*Jeanne McElvaney*

*Three*

# SPEAKING TRUTH

I watched from the second-floor balcony as my strapping young son, Richard, hoisted the extension ladder back onto the rack of his truck. Turning to escape the afternoon sun, I entered the gloom of my newly rented "home," sliding the glass door shut behind me. I eased my aching body onto one of the half-emptied packing boxes near the front door.

*Thank God there are two entrances to this cracker box, and thank God for my son being home when I called, otherwise I would still be sitting outside on the steps in this heat. I can't believe I was stupid enough to lock myself out.*

The front door swung open, and Richard's sturdy frame filled the room. "You gonna be all right, Mom?" Concern spread over his face and began to cloud his eyes.

"Of course. I'm fine."

Rising, I stood with feet apart and crossed my arms in front of me. "I took care of you, your brother, *and* your father for twenty-five years. I can certainly take care of just myself now."

Richard removed his baseball cap, wiped his face on the back of his arm, and put the cap back over his sweaty hair. "Well, I'm as close as a phone call." One of his winning smiles spread across his face. "You know, Mom—you may want to hide a second key somewhere outside, just in case."

"I've already thought of that. I have it on my list."

"I know you can take care of yourself, but you've lost a lot of weight. Mike and I are worried about you."

I dropped my hands to my hips and squared my shoulders. "I'm fine. Just fine. This place is fine." I waved one hand out toward the clutter that surrounded me. "I have the whole summer to rest and gain weight once I get things back to normal. Besides, this apartment will be a piece of cake after caring for that showcase your father is still living in … Everything is perfectly fine."

"Sure, Mom. Just let me know if you need anything." Richard took a stride toward the door then turned. "While I was loading the ladder, I noticed how dirty your car is. You want me to wash it for you? You should have rented a place with a garage."

"Richard, you have a contracting business and a new fiancée to be concerned about. You do *not* need to take care of me, too. Now get out of here so I can get something done—and thank you," I added softly as I opened the door and ushered him out.

The heat outside was stifling. I closed the door quickly then leaned my boney back against it with my hand still on the knob. My mind screamed.

*Back to normal?* I stared around at the unpacked boxes surrounding me. *Nothing will be normal in my life again, even if I do unpack the few things I brought with me. I can't deal with this mess now. I don't even know where to begin.*

My purse sat on the floor in front of me where I had left it—with my keys sitting right on top. I began to relive the terror I'd felt when I realized I'd locked myself out of my new one-bedroom apartment and had no way to get back in, no car keys to go for help, and no way to access a phone to call for help.

*That last load I just had to get from my car—that was my undoing. All I needed to do was remember to release this silly little button on this stupid doorknob.*

I punched and released the offending button on the knob in my hand over and over again as my mind continued to rant.

*Well, don't just stand there feeling sorry for yourself, Carolyn. You figured it out, now do something to put this place in order.*

My body, however, rebelled at the thought of emptying one more box. I slumped down onto the floor and tears flooded my eyes.

*I'll do just one more thing to put my life back in order, then I can rest. Why not take the car to the Super Wash and get it cleaned? That's a sit-down job I can do.*

Soon I found myself inching slowly toward the yawning mouth of the carwash in my tightly closed vehicle. Sweat emerged on my stiff upper lip as the car jerked and bumped forward. I felt strangely vulnerable as the machinery roared into action and the rotating plastic whips slashed against the windshield, just inches from my face. My chest felt like some invisible force was sitting on it. The smell of soap and wax swirled around the humid atmosphere of my car.

I glanced around with relief as the buffeting of the blowers subsided and the track automatically deposited me on the other side of the protective canvas strips that curtained the exit. To my dismay, I noticed some bird droppings still clinging tenaciously to the front windshield. Putting the car in gear, I set the handbrake, grabbed a tissue and got out to wipe off the offending spot.

The next thing I knew a large black truck was suddenly ejected from the exit. I stared helplessly as it collided into the back of my car.

The enraged owner emerged from his vehicle yelling, "What in the hell do you think you're doing, lady!"

As he strode toward me, a million retorts and excuses flashed through my mind, but I let all of them go in a moment of complete surrender.

"Obviously something stupid," was my simple response. "I was wiping off some bird doo-doo." I watched in wide-eyed amazement as this towering behemoth visibly deflated before my very eyes.

"Well … well … don't do that again," he sputtered. Turning, he walked back to his truck without even pausing to check for possible damage. I'm sure I heard him laughing as I got into my car and drove back to the chaos awaiting me in my new home.

My carwash experience was such a revelation. I had always equated power with force, and anger or fear. Before now I could not remember personally experiencing the stunning power of surrender. This episode was helpful in preparing me for my next hurdle—facing Lee when he returned from negotiating the sale of our cabin in Idaho and found me and some of our household possessions gone from the home we had built together.

Having married so young, this was the first time in my forty-five years on the planet I had lived on my own. I was on a steep learning curve regarding autonomy. My first eighteen years were spent with family in my childhood home, then a year and a half in a dormitory at an all-girls' college, and finally another twenty-five years of marriage with a man I loved and trusted to take care of me. This personal history was not particularly conducive to living independently.

I consulted with my Al-Anon advisor, Loren, on how to confront Lee with his betrayal and my decision to leave. How could I possibly tell the man I had shared more than twenty-five years of my life with that I was abandoning him? My "peace at any cost" mentality never allowed me to challenge Lee's authority. My co-dependent nature had (in the Al-Anon vernacular) turned me into a doormat. Doormats do not function independently. They just lay there and get stepped on.

Loren coached me to speak in what she referred to as "I messages," to avoid the "blame game." I was to stick strictly to how I was *feeling,* and avoid bringing up his transgressions from the past.

Her comment was, "Lee can deny or make excuses for your accusations, but he cannot say you don't feel what you feel."

Could it be that simple? Stick to how his behavior made me feel instead of blaming him for behavior I didn't like?

So, how *had* I felt about the events of the past year? I had buried my true feelings so deeply for so long I had no idea how to begin to give voice to how I felt. When I pondered exactly what I might say, I noticed my hand always went to my heart. Was that where my feelings were hidden? Was the pounding of my heart those trapped feelings trying to escape?

Remembering all this, I can only imagine how Lee must have felt when he returned from selling our mountain cabin and found the house empty of the woman he professed to be "unable to live without," along with most of her belongings. Before I made my big decision to take action, we had made the heart-breaking decision to let the cabin go to new owners. The kids were grown and on their own now and, besides, we needed the money since Lee's sick leave was about to expire.

Since I still had to finish out the school year, I had sent him on this mission to Idaho without saying a word about my intention to finally carry through on the consequence I had threatened some months before. I made this cowardly decision because I could not bear the thought of having him fuming and mumbling as I packed up my things and moved out.

Upon his return, the boys told their father my new phone number, and Lee called me to request a meeting. Never in my life have I been as apprehensive as when I walked back into the home I had just abandoned. I do not remember exactly what I said to him, but I do remember I was careful to stick with "I messages"—how I felt about where we were now in our life together. I stuck with my feelings and simply spoke from my heart. It worked, just as it had done with the driver of the truck I encountered at the Super Wash. There were no excuses, no denials, and no argument on Lee's part. He listened quietly to what I had to say, then asked if he could help me with anything and whether I needed something more from the house.

I also remember I had said I wanted a legal separation. I intentionally did not use the "D" word. I held onto the belief that Lee's love for me was so strong he would surely quit drinking to get me back and then we could resume our life together. I seriously underestimated the depth of his disease.

*Vulnerability sounds like truth and feels like courage.*
*Truth and courage aren't always comfortable,*
*but they are never weakness.*

—*Brené Brown*

*Four*

# LONELINESS

Before school let out for the summer I had some high hurdles to leap. My first dreaded task after my separation was to inform my father and other family members about my failing marriage. Leaving your marriage was unprecedented in the Bourns family. The part of me that always strived toward perfection was having a hard time reconciling what I believed to be a moral failure. For a people pleaser like me, the thought of my father's disapproval terrified me as I picked up the receiver and dialed my childhood phone number.

After exchanging pleasantries, I admitted to my father what I had just done, shared my new address and phone number, then waited for the lecture. I did not mention Lee's drinking as my reason for taking this unprecedented step, so I was stunned by his response.

"Carolyn, there is no greater stress and no greater hell than spending a lifetime living with an alcoholic. I discovered quite some time ago that if I chose not to take that first drink for the day, alcohol was not a problem. This realization has helped me and many of my patients to stop drinking."

I was shocked, yet relieved and deeply grateful, by his compassionate words. Shocking was the realization that my father (and by extension probably the whole family) was well aware of the dirty little secret I had done everything in my power to conceal. I had failed miserably at my co-dependent job as keeper of the family secret and protector of my alcoholic loved one from public exposure and ridicule.

Just in case I hadn't gotten that message, a second encounter confirmed this big reveal. The news of our separation had traveled quickly within the school where I taught. I met a staff member in the hallway to the faculty room one morning. Lee and I had known and socialized with Pat and her husband for years. She had recently transferred from Lee's school to mine. In the shame and embarrassment of my recent separation, I felt compelled to apologize and explain. I don't remember my words to her, but I do remember her exact response.

"Carolyn, you owe no one an explanation or an apology. We were all just wondering what took you so long."

If I had to use just one word to describe my experience of that first six months in my new little apartment, it would be loneliness. I never had great numbers of people pounding at my door seeking my companionship, but there had always been family, neighbors, and teaching associates. I closed out the school year, completed organizing and decorating my tiny living space, and then looked around for what to do next.

Every year for the past fifteen years, my summers had been spent in Idaho at the cabin. Island Park, Idaho is an oasis in the High Rockies. That area is the headwaters of the Snake River and our cabin was only a few miles from Big Springs, where you could stand on a bridge and look into the pristine depths to see rainbow trout seemingly as big as tuna. These amazing creatures would spawn in the crystalline waters of the spring and supply fingerling fry that grew to populate the trophy fishing tributaries downstream. Some of these tiny creatures eventually made their way to the Columbia River and out to the ocean to become steelhead, then took their long and arduous journey back upstream to spawn again at Big Springs.

We had purchased our little A-frame cabin on a whim. The first year we took the camper to that area to visit, we stayed at a lovely campground near Mack's Inn. Lee had two teaching colleagues who owned summer cabins in the area. When they were visiting our campsite one evening, the conversation drifted to what would be the absolute requirement for a mountain cabin if you owned one. My immediate response was that it would have to have a big, lovely fireplace.

"That's interesting," one of our visitors responded. "My cousin wants to sell his cabin near Box Canyon and the Buffalo River. It has an amazing fireplace."

Well, it was love at first sight, but that was because of the two features that enticed us to take a look at the property—the location and the fireplace. The cabin itself was completely unfinished inside, with only an outhouse behind. The design for its construction was what is called a double A-frame. This means it is all roof with very little interior. However, the great benefit of an A-frame is that we didn't have the worry of cutting snow off a flat or even a pitched roof in winter. There was space for a small kitchen downstairs; a huge native-rock fireplace was the centerpiece of a combined living and dining room area; and a ladder led up to an empty loft that would eventually accommodate a platform bed, closet, and tiny bathroom with stall shower.

Even though we got the cabin at what Californians considered a heck of a deal, the improvements were costly, beginning with the drilling of a well so we could have indoor plumbing instead of hauling water. It took years to complete the upgrades, but eventually our cabin in the woods became a cozy and comfortable summer retreat.

More than just the cabin and the fishing, however, were the people we met and the friends we made in the area. Many in the valley below would drive out of the heat to their mountain cabins to get away from it all. This usually meant endless cookouts, round-ups, and potlucks. I became very close and involved with a lovely group of women. We formed what was to become The Island Park Ladies' Golf Association. The local golf course was pretty scruffy, but it was close by and none of us were very good golfers anyway. Every year we would plan an overnight trip we referred to as our annual "run-away" to a nearby premiere golf course: Sun Valley, the Grand Tetons, or up along the Gallatin Canyon to Big Sky or Bozeman. Golf was actually ancillary to the fun of getting away from our husbands and domestic duties for a day or two. In fact, our association president didn't even play golf; Julia simply had senior status and loved to entertain us after our round.

⟿

Feeling lonely and at loose ends that first summer of my separation, I decided I needed the companionship, nurturing, and fun of being with my golfing buddies. The cabin was sold and gone, so I made arrangements with one of the ladies to stay with her and her husband for a week. Bob and Alice had raised eight children who were now married and raising children of their own. In fact, the summer before, I had helped Alice finish sewing a going-away outfit for the August wedding of one of her daughters. I wouldn't say the Bowers's residence in Island Park was exactly a cabin, even though it was log construction. The structure had been in their family for generations and easily accommodated a horde, so I knew there would be a spare bed for me now that so many of their "chicks" had flown the nest.

My next challenge was navigating the approximately one thousand mile trip over the High Sierras, through the Nevada desert, east along the Snake River, then north at Pocatello toward the west entrance to Yellowstone Park in Montana. I had made that trip so many times over the years, but never did the driving. Lee always insisted on driving, no matter where we went together and for however long we drove. The truck and camper were his domain. Undaunted by the ordeal ahead of me, I packed a bag and set out for Idaho.

As American author Thomas Wolfe is famous for saying, "You can't go home again." Nothing was the same, and I felt others' judgement of my decision to separate from my marriage. A solo woman was simply not welcome in this vacation atmosphere, and I was totally at a loss to know what to do with myself. Most of my time was spent walking the streams nearby, catching trout, or going to Huckleberry Hill to pick enough fruit for pie or cereal in an attempt to "earn my keep" and stay out of the way.

I was relegated to the huge upstairs loft where the children and grandchildren slept when they visited. It was terribly hot up there during the day, so I had to sneak downstairs to find a cool comfortable corner to read. About five days into my visit, the clincher to my discomfort was overhearing a phone conversation Alice was having out in the kitchen with someone (possibly one of the other golf ladies).

"I don't know when she's planning on leaving, and I *really* don't know what to do with her. I just want the place to myself before the kids start coming with the grandkids."

*Why hadn't she said something? Was she just being dramatic, or had I become the pest she was describing to the person on the other end of the line?*

Needless to say, I was beyond embarrassed. I was mortified! I had become an imposition, no matter how hard I tried to contribute and to stay out of the way. I snuck back up to the loft, packed my bag, and wrote a very proper note telling the Bowers how much I had appreciated their kind hospitality. When Alice left on her errands for the day, I placed the note on kitchen counter, threw my bag in the car, and headed south, back to California. Indeed, I could not go back to my old stomping grounds and act like nothing had changed. It was time for me to look forward and start crafting a new life.

That thousand-mile drive back to Walnut Creek provided plenty of time for reflection. First, of course, my inner critic started screaming at me, telling me all the things I should have, could have, would have said and done, instead of the cowardly way I handled my feelings and slunk away.

Once I tired of beating myself up, I turned my attention to the next project awaiting me back home. I had been hired for a part-time job by the Concord Department of Leisure Services that would start in August. When I was plotting my separation plan, I had deep concern over how I would be able to support myself on only my teaching salary, even though I was at the top of the district pay scale. I applied for a newly created position as program coordinator for an after-school program to address the needs of so-called "latch-key kids." The city of Concord previously conducted a study to see what aspect of the community was being underserved, and this was the demographic that surfaced.

I had great passion for the cause because I taught this exact age group. At the time, the prevailing thinking by a majority of parents was that once your child entered fourth grade, they were perfectly capable of being on their own after school under certain conditions. These children, as young as nine, were expected to come straight home after school, unlock the door, then let themselves into an empty house. They were not to let anyone in until their mom or dad got home to supervise. As far as I was concerned, these kids should be outside playing with their peers and blowing off excess stored energy from their hours in the classroom. They needed a nutritious snack, a "motherly" type to help them with their homework and soothe their worries, as well as an older teen or college student to supervise after-school play. I was excited at the prospect of creating a program to meet these needs.

I will admit, however, that the biggest motivation for taking on a second job was not my idealism, nor my passion. Rather, it was my ignorance concerning how much money I would have to earn to take care of myself now that I would be living on my own. Lee and I got married and tried to finish our educations on an unemployment check, so I had learned how to be extremely frugal during our first years of married life. All funding for my education ceased when Lee and I eloped to Reno to get married. Lee was finishing his final year at the University of California in Berkeley, doing swing-shift work at Lucky Lager Brewing Company on a part-time basis. Swing shift at a brewery was the perfect job for someone working his way through college. Lee could draw unemployment when he was laid off and not earning a salary. That allowed him to take a full load at the university if he scheduled morning and early afternoon classes. It also allowed for a refrigerator full of beer that came home in his lunch pail each evening.

Because he was the main wage-earner in the family, Lee always handled the finances and we had one joint account, even when I became a full-time teacher in 1965. Since it was not particularly common at that time for married women with children to continue working, I was somewhat of a trendsetter for my generation, but still heavily influenced by my parents' model of home and family. When I was nearing high school graduation, my father sat me down and asked me if I wanted to get married and raise a family, *or* did I want to go on to college and have a career. My desire to do both was not an option as far as Dad was concerned. Since I had no boyfriend at the time, I made the obvious decision and started applying to different colleges in California. I had dreamed of living in that sunny state ever since I had visited there with my cousins my sophomore year in high school.

When I got back to the apartment, I set right to work, determined to keep busy with my new project. I named the program Our House and set about contacting administrators of the different elementary schools in Concord to see if they were interested in participating. Six of the eight school administrators within the Concord city limits said yes. My next task was to find and hire for each site a motherly or grandmotherly type and a college student type who wanted a part-time position and loved fourth, fifth, and sixth graders. The next step was to set up the curriculum for the program, and design and distribute the materials to promote the program within each school's attendance area. I also made arrangements for the city's food pantry to commit to making healthy snacks available.

All was going smoothly until it got to the pièce de résistance of my vision for Our House. It always touched my heart, when I drove to and from school, to see the senior crossing guards at busy intersections as they interacted so lovingly with the kids in their charge. The children encircled their guardian for many light changes before they headed off for school or home. I had also noticed a trend toward isolating the elders of our community and relegating them to gated communities and other facilities out of sight from the general population. It was as though the baby boomers did not want to be reminded that they too were going to get old. Here were two factions of my community that were being disenfranchised. Why not bring the wisdom of the elderly together with the loneliness of the latch-key kids within the city? I imagined the women teaching such skills as crafts, cooking, and sewing and the men initiating carpentry, board games, science experiments, and other important life skills.

So, I prepared my proposal and sat down with Ed, the Director of Leisure Services. I knew he also directed the seniors' program for the city, so he would surely see this as a fabulous opportunity to enhance both programs.

I was sadly disappointed by his response. "Carolyn, the seniors already have a full program with plenty of activities to keep them busy. They wouldn't be interested in anything like this."

Undaunted, I replied, "It won't hurt to ask them. This would be a strictly voluntary activity. At least we can place the opportunity before them and let them decide for themselves if this is something they'd like to do."

"We'll see," was the reply. I never heard back from Ed on the matter.

My second rejection was lobbying for higher wages for the two supervisors I would be placing at each site. I knew the success of the program would depend upon attracting and keeping good people. I could provide an interesting curriculum, gather materials, and lend support, but these employees were the front line and the heart of the program. Again, my request fell on deaf ears. It seemed there were classifications and a pre-determined pay scale with no wiggle room for exceptions, no matter how great the responsibility of the position. So much for creativity and flexibility within a bureaucracy.

When school started in the fall, my classroom was decorated and ready to go and so was the Our House after-school program for fourth, fifth, and sixth graders at six schools in Concord. I was extremely busy, but I still went home to an empty apartment each night and was terribly lonely. Most of the people I might socialize with were married, and the reality of a two-by-two world clutched at my heart. I did continue my Al-Anon support group meetings with Loren and looked forward to the one night each week of companionship, comfort, and support the members provided.

Lee called and visited me occasionally, bringing strange gifts of appeasement—an antique oak desk and chair, a heart-shaped ceramic pin with the word "love" on it, a set of opal earrings—but there was still no indication of his sobriety and he had not been reinstated by the school district. Word reached me that he was telling all his acquaintances that I left him due to being influenced and seduced by a religious cult. If this was his belief about Al-Anon, it gave me some insight into his absolute refusal to attend the spiritually based AA meetings in the area. Lee confused religion with spirituality. Religious cults through the sixties and seventies enticed such luminaries as Patty Hearst, the granddaughter of the wealthy and famous newspaper founder William Randolph Hearst, away from their families and loved ones. Since this was the mid-eighties, Lee's story was a face-saving and somewhat believable tactic.

I learned my lesson in Idaho. You can't go back. The denial finally lifted and the path became clear. Lee's love and need for alcohol was greater than his love for me. A few months into the school term, we began divorce proceedings. Lee insisted on being the one to file, and I was fine with that. All I wanted to do was move forward in my life, not back.

*Negative emotions like loneliness,*
*envy and guilt have an important role to play in a happy life.*
*They're flashing signs that something needs to change.*

*—Gretchen Rubin*

*Five*

# REENTRY

Well, Plan A (he'll get sober and we can resume our life together) was a dismal failure. The dissolution settlement moved forward: Lee got the truck and camper, the monthly payments coming from the recent sale of the cabin, and half the equity from the sale of our home; I got the car, the tax-shelter annuities, and the other half of the amount received when the house sold. All the structures we had worked so hard to build together collapsed with the stroke of a pen as the divorce papers were agreed upon and signed. Lee stalled about putting the house on the market, but I was much too busy with a full *and* a part-time job to push the matter.

Soon, however, my evening isolation and desire to join in on social activities began to get the better of me. I cast about for a solution. It had not escaped my notice that a number of my teaching colleagues were now on second marriages that seemed to be working out very well for them. I would choose more carefully this time, but where to begin?

My daily activities exposed me pretty exclusively to women and children. There was next to no opportunity to meet "Mr. Right" in an elementary school setting. I was at a loss to know how to proceed. I had not dated since high school, over a quarter of a century before, so my flirting skills were extremely rusty. A chance meeting in the grocery store or other public place seemed remote. There was no such thing as home computers and online dating services in the eighties. Some magazines and newspapers devoted a small portion of their classified ads to connecting singles. But can you imagine?

### Lonely in Walnut Creek

45-year old single female seeking male companionship. Must be financially stable and willing to take care of me for the rest of my life. Call: xxx-xxx-xxxx

It was crystal clear to me. I was not about to risk that kind of exposure and make public my wants, needs, and phone number. Placing an ad in my local newspaper, or any other type of publication, was *not* an option.

One evening while attending my weekly Al-Anon support meeting, I shared my dilemma with the group. I noticed Loren giving the woman who co-facilitated with her a conspiratorial look. The two seemed to reach some sort of silent agreement. Loren then turned to me and asked if I would meet with her briefly when we finished group.

"Carolyn," Loren explained kindly after the meeting, "I was reluctant to share this information with the whole group present. Facilitators are cautioned not to get involved with the personal affairs of the group participants. Betty and I feel, however, you have been in Al-Anon long enough and worked on yourself hard enough for me to share a resource you may want to explore. There is a large Presbyterian church here in the central county that has a program to help singles meet in a safe and fun environment. I'll bring the name and contact information for you to next week's meeting."

I fairly floated out of the building. On the drive home, thoughts danced inside my head. I was thrilled to know a community resource, much like the new program I was creating for latch-key kids, had been formed to address the needs of another growing demographic that felt isolated from the mainstream. I was grateful to Loren for having the compassion to bend rules and share this information with me. Now I would have a safe and more comfortable way to "mix and mingle" with available and appropriate men. Thus began my foray out into uncharted territory to initiate Plan B.

I called the number Loren gave me the very next week and was sent materials that detailed the beginning steps necessary to become a participating member of the LOPC Singles Organization. The mailer described it as "friendly and open social groups, known as 'ships,' that offer an opportunity to make friends and to share fun, food, fellowship, and service." I noted the date and location for the next general gathering and orientation, then resolved to attend while butterflies cavorted in my gut.

*I wish I had someone else to go with me, but everyone I know is married, so that's not an option. I'll go by myself and just get more information. I certainly don't have to commit to anything that doesn't seem safe.*

I have often joked with friends and acquaintances that I must have been trampled to death by a crowd in a past life. You see, I suffer from enochlophobia—a fear of crowds. I am mildly anxious when in a crowded room with others I know. I was soon to find out that this mild anxiety could turn into a full-blown panic attack if I was by myself in a crush of unfamiliar people. I was so protected most of my life that I had no idea this discomfort could lead to shaking, trembling, excessive sweating, and a feeling of being unable to breathe.

On the evening of the orientation, I found my way to the church perched high up in the Las Trampas hills, not all that far from where I now lived in Walnut Creek. The worship hall itself was dwarfed by the outbuildings and activities auditorium nearby. I knew I was in trouble from the get-go. The parking lot was completely full, and vehicles lined the steep and winding streets for blocks. My first hurdle was to locate a parking spot and then find my way back to the church. I followed the gathering crowd as we made our way to the huge community room for the general meeting. I hovered toward the back of the standing-room-only crowd as we were greeted.

After a short welcoming speech, newcomers were instructed to go to a nearby classroom according to our assigned group. Three groups had been formed to meet the needs of the different ages: those born in 1939 and before were Singleships; 1940 to 1955 were Shipmates; 1956 and after were Voyagers. My assigned group, Shipmates, was definitely the largest and consisted mainly of baby boomers. The standard-size classroom where we met for orientation was filled to capacity, again with standing room only. They had these meetings once a month, for god's sake. It was becoming apparent to me that there was nothing unique within my larger community about my singleness.

I left that night with a Shipmates' newsletter naming and describing the myriad of activities one could choose from to get started. As I pored over the next month's offerings, one particular event caught my attention—a dance. When I was in high school, my mother insisted I attend Mary Ann Wells' Dance Studio in Seattle to learn ballroom dancing. At first I hated it, because I didn't know any of the kids and was soon to discover I had very poor body memory for the steps required to pull off the different types and styles of ballroom dancing. Fox-trot, quickstep, swing, and waltz were okay. But the Latin dances like tango, rumba, and cha-cha I never mastered. However, I stuck with it and soon became very skilled at following a good lead. Despite my height, I was lithe and light on my feet, so eventually I attracted a small group of very good dance partners. Later in my dancing history, Lee and I loved to swing dance together and would often be applauded by appreciative spectators. After reviewing the failures and successes in my mind, I began building a rationale for my selection. My reasoning went something like this:

*I'm still fit and trim and not too hard to look at. I love to dance and, if we're busy dancing, I won't have to struggle with striking up and maintaining a conversation with someone I don't know. I think I'll go out and buy a new dress and shoes for the occasion.*

So, I signed up to attend the event, which was to take place the middle of November, then found the time to go out and buy a new outfit for my reentry into the dating scene. As I recall, it was a blue and white belted plaid dress with three-quarter length sleeves and a full skirt (the sort of thing Donna Reed might have worn in her 1950s TV series). I pictured in my mind how it would flare out dramatically when I was pushed out and twirled on the dance floor by my partner. This was going to be great fun.

The big night arrived, and I took my time getting ready. I didn't want to arrive too early and be seen standing all by myself, looking awkward. I decided to wait until the crowd gathered and was fully occupied by the dancing, then make my entrance unnoticed. Again, there was a problem finding a parking spot, and I had to walk quite a distance in the dark to get to the community center where the event was being held. There was no problem finding my way, however. The earsplitting music carried for blocks.

I soon discovered that my new outfit was a huge mistake. It was the era of tights and leg warmers, miniskirts, and palazzo pants. I needn't have worried about not mastering the Latin dances. Now I had the many moves of the salsa to learn, along with the hustle, the bump, YMCA, the funky chicken, and different line-dancing moves. It was simply overwhelming. I watched for a while from the back of the "wallflower line," feeling phobic and self-conscious. Soon I fled back to the solitude and safety of my apartment. I never wore that plaid dress again.

Not to be daunted, I pulled out the Shipmates' newsletter and scanned the remaining events for the month. Obviously, large group gatherings were not "my cup of tea," so I selected a weekend excursion to Sea Ranch, located up north in Sonoma County for my next adventure. A large home was rented for us to share, and the locale provided the opportunity to walk the beach, play golf, and hang out with other select singles in a lovely setting. When I called to sign up, I was paired with Faye, another single living in my same city. We could carpool and share sleeping quarters. How perfect was that? This gave me the opportunity to meet someone my age and gender who was also single. As it turned out, most of the participants for this event were women. The men who did attend were quite a bit younger than me. Faye and I became fast friends, however, and our relationship continued for years, even after she found her "Mr. Right" and married him.

I got my sea legs on the vessel Shipmates and soon discovered most of the men my age and older were there to find a younger woman. They ignored the orientation rules concerning members' assigned group according to age and were now seeking greener pastures. Not being any kind of a swinger and definitely being one of the oldest on the ship, I decided to join in on the activities with the old fogies in Singleship.

Soon I started dating different men I met, usually while attending small house parties hosted by different people in the Singleship group who owned large homes. I was awkward and uncomfortable with the drink-in-hand, mix-and-mingle thing, but I'm very handy in the kitchen. I discovered if I helped the host or hostess, it gave me an opportunity to become a part of the evening's activity and engage more comfortably in conversation. It wasn't long before I became intimate with a few of the men I dated—which was always a great disappointment. With a full-time teaching position, a part-time job after school, and my weekends taken up with social activities, I was exhausted.

One rainy morning in early February, I woke up feeling just awful. I had a fever and searing pain running up my right leg and into my groin. I stumbled out of bed and into the bathroom, seeking something in the medicine chest that I could take to ease my symptoms. After downing two aspirin, I decided a warm bath might help, and then I could crawl back into bed and sweat the thing out, whatever it was. To my dismay, no matter how long I ran the water, it remained ice cold, so I crawled back into bed and waited for the discomfort to go away. It just got worse. I called my building manager and reported the problem with the hot water. Her reply was that it must be that the water heater had broken, but she could not get anyone out to fix it until Monday. It was Saturday morning.

Eventually, I struggled out of bed, threw on some clothes, and set out to see a doctor. I had medical insurance through the school district, but had recently changed my provider. I was seldom sick and only used my coverage for wellness checks, so during the open enrollment I had switched to a new HMO that was affiliated with the county hospital. Unfortunately, I had not yet gotten around to selecting a primary care physician with my new plan. My only option was to go to medical emergency and take potluck. This did not especially thrill me as the problem appeared to be in a very private area of my body.

I will spare you the gruesome details, but my first time "out of the barn," so to speak, I contracted what turned out to be genital herpes. I was misdiagnosed, however, and treated instead for pelvic inflammatory disease with a month's course of very powerful antibiotics. Since I had a viral infection, the bacteria killer had no place to go other than do massive damage to the lining of my intestines and bladder.

So much for Plan B. I was damaged goods, and no man would ever want me now. As I turned self-loathing and shame in on myself for ruining my life, the dis-ease and gut-wrenching pain continued to escalate.

The diagnoses were many, the conclusion the same: "Your condition is chronic and irreversible, Mrs. Odom. You will just have to learn to live with it."

*Fall in love when you're ready, not when you're lonely.*

—*Vanga Srikanth*

*Six*

# PEACE OF MIND

There's a saying in my family: *it never rains but it pours*. Shortly after I was told by the doctors they couldn't help me, I received a very official looking letter from Lee's lawyer reminding me of my agreed-upon obligation to share the tax bill for 1985. I was stunned by the amount that was due by mid-April. Both Lee and I were salaried, with taxes automatically withdrawn by our employers. However, two things had changed for the last tax period: first, my earnings for half the year from my part-time job put us in a whole other tax bracket (agreeing to file jointly was a huge mistake); second, Lee took out a second mortgage to consolidate and pay off credit card debt. Somehow we owed money on that immediately even though we would get most of it back when the home sold. Paying my part of the amount owed would completely wipe out my meager bank account, and then some.

There were four long months remaining to the end of the school year. The physical pain I was now experiencing 24-7 due to my damaged intestines drained my energy and made it next to impossible to get a good night's sleep. I also lost a lot of weight because digesting food was such a difficult task for my tender gut. My time in the classroom, which used to be joyful and rewarding, now became a herculean task as I struggled to keep up with the curriculum and needs of thirty-one third and fourth graders in my combination class. After work, I dragged myself to the car and raced around to the different school sites, bringing snacks and equipment for the Our House program. It was an almost unbearable day if I had to stand in and substitute for an absent supervisor on one of the sites. If I was not trying to meet my commitments to my full and part-time jobs, then I was in my apartment cleaning, correcting student papers, and trying to recover sufficiently to make it through another week.

For years, teachers in the upper elementary (fourth through sixth) grades had been subsidizing the rest of the district for the sake of a better education for the children we were committed to teach. Our sacrifice of extra time each day with the children in the classroom helped pay for aides and a smaller class size for grades kindergarten through third and for the prep periods for all the intermediate and high school teachers. Granted, we probably had the easiest age group to teach, but upper elementary teachers had larger class sizes and longer hours, with all the students present for the entire day. The one twenty-minute break we did get in the morning was, more often than not, taken up with supporting individual students or supervising the yard. Attending to my personal needs throughout most of the day was not an option.

Fortunately, state law required that all teachers have a half hour duty-free lunch break, but I often commented I felt more like a camel than a human. If I was assigned "yard duty" for the week, it was almost four hours until that noon break came along. Drinking the copious amounts of water now required to keep my intestines and bladder even slightly happy was not possible during school hours. State law also required that a credentialed adult be present at all times when children were in the classroom. Proper hydration and access to a bathroom was not much of a consideration for upper elementary school teachers. It was simply not in the budget.

If I could hold on until the end of the school year, I reasoned, I would have the whole summer to rest and recover. Another option presented itself that was tempting. One of the other fifth grade teachers was due to return next school year after taking a maternity leave. However, she did not want to teach full time and was looking for someone to job-share with her. I thought highly of Shirley and this seemed an interesting opportunity coming up at this time. However, I couldn't imagine surviving on only half salary.

The time had come for me to launch Plan C, so I could manage my life more predictively. My father had withdrawn all financial support the minute I got married over twenty-five years ago. I was single now and in poor health. Could I count on his financial help if I needed it? Would my stepmother, Eve, approve if I asked Dad for a loan to handle the tax matter? If the doctors here in my area couldn't offer me any solutions, could my father the doctor recommend a specialist or protocol that would cure me? Easter vacation was coming at the end of March. That would be the perfect time to approach him on these matters. So, I called and Dad said he and Eve would be delighted to see me any time. I booked my flight to Seattle immediately.

In the meantime life went on. My new "home" was in a complex known as the Camelback Apartments. It occupied approximately a full block, with nicely landscaped courtyards between each of the numerous two-story fourplexes. There was a pool and laundry facility for tenants not too far from my building. One weekend, while I was doing my laundry, I happened to notice a paperback left on one of the folding tables. I was intrigued by the title: *Teach Only Love: Transform your Life with the Seven Principles of Attitudinal Healing* by Gerald Jampolsky, M.D. Well, that caught my attention. What in heaven's name did one's attitude have to do with repairing the physical cells of the body? In my estimation, the fact that a medical doctor had authored the book gave it more credibility, so I investigated further. Upon scanning the introduction, I discovered the author had compiled these principles from a larger body of work known as *A Course in Miracles*. A miracle was exactly what it was going to take to get me out of my present pickle. I flipped through the book to find the list of principles, so I could get started.

I was completely stymied by the first—and, according to the good doctor, the most important—principle. *"Peace of mind as an instrument of transformation: it can be a powerful tool for anyone, from those dealing with everyday problems to those with life-threatening illnesses."*

I was still not convinced that my myriad of symptoms and diagnosed conditions had anything to do with my mind. After all, had I not been the victim of a wrong diagnosis and given the incorrect medication? Wasn't that what had ruined my health? Besides, I didn't have a clue where to begin to clear and quiet my mind when my focus was on surviving. I set the book back on the table, vowing to buy my own copy so I could read the whole thing.

The next interesting synchronicity to occur was the contents of a package that arrived in the mail from my aunt. Her given name was Carolyn, and I had been named after Aunt Care by my mother. Mom was the youngest of three sisters; Helen was next (we called her Aunt Feathers), and Care was the oldest. All the women on my mother's side of the family lived into their mid-nineties, so it came as a huge shock to everyone when Mom was diagnosed with ovarian cancer at the age of sixty-three. She died within four short months of the discovery of numerous tumors filling her abdomen. Never married and having no children of her own, my dear Aunt Care stepped into the void my mother left with her passing. I referred to her as my surrogate mom and, since I had gotten sick, she made a point to call me at least once a week for support. Of course, she would say it was just to talk, but I knew she was worried about me.

When I tore open the package, I saw that Aunt Care had sent me a book. The note enclosed explained that a new little shop had recently opened in "the village" (our name for the little town of Winslow on Bainbridge Island, where I grew up). She went on to elaborate that the shop had all kinds of unusual little items like crystals and other gemstones and exotic knickknacks. The store also had a metaphysical book section. Care told the shopkeeper a little about what was going on with me, and this was the book they mutually selected. Aunt Care wrote she hadn't read it, but she really liked the big colorful heart on the cover.

The book was *You Can Heal Your Life* by Louise Hay. The author's key message: "If we are willing to do the mental work, almost anything can be healed." Here was that same message once again—heal your mind and you heal your body. My mind was a Nazi and the inner critic kept abusing me horribly as I relived the guilt of leaving a sick husband and the shame of having contracted a social disease. What could I possibly do now to change any of that? According to the author, we needed to replace negative thoughts with positive words called affirmations. She devoted most of the pages to naming physical ailments and the new thoughts that could be repeated to effect a physical change and heal your body's response to negative events outside your ability to control.

Some of these ideas are as old as time, but for me in the eighties, this was revolutionary. I was skeptical, but I had nothing to lose but my misery, so I turned my attention to creating an affirmation that would embrace both of the books that landed in my lap rather mysteriously. My mantra became, "Deep peace infills me and radiates from me." I followed the rules. My affirmation was in the first person, present tense, and easy to remember. I repeated it over and over to replace the "should have, could have, would have" voice that beleaguered me when I was not focused on my daily activities. Every stop light while driving was a signal to repeat my affirmation.

In my Al-Anon support group we were studying the twelve steps of the "big book" of Alcoholics Anonymous. One evening we were discussing step eleven: "Sought through prayer and meditation to improve our conscious contact with God as we understood Him, praying only for knowledge of His will for us and the power to carry that out." I understood prayer, but I was having a huge problem with the word 'meditation.' Remember, I lived through the era of the '70s, with its cults, abductions, and mass murders. California, as my family back in Washington State kept reminding me, was known for its unusually large number of cults and dodgy religious movements. You could hardly make your way through an airport back in those days without being solicited by a Hare Krishna follower in a saffron robe carrying a stick of smoldering incense. I always equated meditation with Eastern and Middle Eastern religious groups, so I felt very uncomfortable with the word meditation being in the literature of the twelve-step programs. Possibly Lee was right, and I had been captured by a religious cult.

When I expressed my concerns, Loren explained, "Carolyn, prayer is talking to your higher power and meditation is simply clearing your chattering mind, so you can listen to what your higher power has to say in response to your petition."

Well, that was intriguing. "Do you mean that a disembodied entity will actually speak to me, if I learn to meditate?"

"Not necessarily, although for some people it may take the form of their inner ear hearing spoken words or short phrases. For others, it may simply be a feeling sensed in their body that evokes a comfortable or uncomfortable emotion. Still others may actually visualize a symbol or short scene that has meaning for them—sort of like the images we 'see' in our minds' eye when we dream, or it could be some combination of all three."

"But how do we know if it's divine guidance? My mind is conjuring up words, scenarios, and feelings constantly. How can I distinguish between what is a message coming from my ego's thoughts and one from a higher wisdom?"

Loren returned my question with one of her own. "What does surrender and trust mean to you, Carolyn?"

I thought about that for a minute then replied, "Surrender seems like a point of weakness, like I'm giving something up to someone or something. Trust, to me, is relying on someone else to take care of me or help me care for something I value."

"The eleventh step," Loren replied, "is asking us to give up the need to control the things outside ourselves and go inside to connect to a higher authority. Although you have never been taught this, humans are multidimensional beings with gifts and abilities we have yet to fully explore. There are whole new worlds to discover by having the trust to take what some term the inner journey."

Although mystical, Loren's response felt peaceful and reassuring. She sent us home that night with a list of resources to get us started, if we were interested in learning to meditate. Initially, I chose to begin with a cassette tape recording I purchased at B. Dalton Booksellers. I went out and found a lovely little antique rocker with comfortable cushions to use in my bedroom. It occupied the quiet corner by a window looking out on the courtyard below. This became my designated meditation space.

My daily ritual began with a hot shower, dressing, and grooming. Next, I would turn on the tape player, sit in my rocker with feet flat on the floor, close my eyes, then focus on the words coming from the speaker as my breathing slowed. When the tape ended, I would take a few more minutes to recite my affirmation: "Deep peace infills me and radiates from me." I didn't feel anything changing, but I noticed when I focused on the words in the guided meditation, the pain lessened or completely disappeared. However, the minute I resumed my daily activities, all my symptoms returned. Although my symptoms weren't lessened during my workday, two different faculty members on separate occasions asked me what I was doing lately because I seemed so much more peaceful now. Do you suppose my affirmation was beginning to take effect?

Easter vacation finally came, and I was on my way to Washington. I was excited to see my father because I hadn't visited for some time. Dad had received a diagnosis of colon cancer about a year and a half before. The last time I visited was right after his surgery. Doctors were able to remove all of the tumor and the resection had been successful, but malignancy had spread to his liver. Although my mother wasn't able to tolerate chemotherapy many years back, Dad went through it with flying colors and his cancer was now in remission.

My father married Eve about two years after my mother's death. She was an accounting employee in his office for years and recently widowed as well. Initially, I was delighted Dad would now have someone to look after his needs. I remember visiting Mom shortly before she died and being very upset with her because she had given up all treatment and was peacefully waiting to, as she put it, "meet her maker." I implored her to fight the cancer raging through her body. I will never forget her reply.

"Carolyn, I'm ready to go home. My one regret is leaving your father. I don't know what he'll do without me."

Fighting back tears, I reassured her we would visit frequently and I would see he had love, food, and good clothes. For the two years after her death, I made frequent flights up to check on him, or the family and I would make the long drive from California or Idaho to Bainbridge to fill the freezer with food and make sure Dad's needs were met.

About nine years after their marriage, my father and stepmother sold "the big house" (our term for the house we'd grown up in ever since my baby boomer brother, Tom, was born in 1948). Eve's small family home near Winslow had been remodeled, and that was where they would now live.

Over the years, my father had filled every spare space in the big house with his interests and hobbies. The separate two-car garage was filled with his vast tool collection. None of his or Mom's cars had ever seen the inside of that building. He had three of every tool known to man, and then some that were not known because he thought up and crafted them on a metal lathe that was his pride and joy. The large enclosed front porch of the house was occupied with a regulation pool table and a large telescope Dad built himself to study the stars and planets. And the entire attic was taken up with his Lionel train collection, consisting of cars and engines he had been collecting since his childhood. It was inconceivable to imagine all of this could be dismantled and consolidated to fit the small home they would be occupying.

Dad gave away or sold most of his tools, his enormous train collection, and the pool table. At the same time he requested that Barney, Tom, and I come to the house and take anything we wanted that Eve didn't want for her house. On that particular trip, I went upstairs and took a look in my childhood bedroom. There in a corner, I spotted the upholstered antique rocker that Mom and Dad had in their bedroom downstairs for as long as I could remember. After Dad married Eve, it had evidently been relegated to a corner of my empty bedroom. That was the only item I could see left in the house that I cared about. I called my father upstairs, showed him the rocker, and said that if Eve didn't want to use it, I would like to have it.

I remember I was stunned by his reply, "Are you sure it's our rocker? That it doesn't belong to Eve?"

My father was so oblivious to the amenities around him that he did not recognize a piece of furniture he'd walked around in his bedroom for some forty years. I reassured him that Aunt Care had asked about the rocker, and said it had been one of the family antiques she and my grandmother had given Mom shortly after she and Dad were married. Dad never got back to me on the rocker, so I decided to let the matter drop.

Imagine how I felt when I walked through the front room of their newly renovated home and saw Mom's rocker. It was now catapulted to a place of honor next to one of Eve's family rockers. Such a little thing. It was just a piece of furniture, for god's sake. But to me, symbolically, it represented more of what could never be ever again. It felt like I had been jabbed through my heart.

The next blow was delivered after our dinner. I sat down alone with Dad and told him I had been diagnosed with something called interstitial cystitis. Evidently, the antibiotic had burned my bladder so badly, it had caused the protective coating lining the bladder to form cracks that weren't healing. Now urine seeped through these cracks into the delicate interstitial tissue below and caused severe pain and the constant urgency to void. At its worst, it felt like a knife jabbing and twisting right behind my pubic bone.

My father looked at me with the greatest compassion. "That must be horrible, Carolyn, but I've never heard of this kind of cystitis before." No help there.

The loan, however, was not a problem, and he asked how much I needed to cover my tax obligations. He immediately wrote me a check for the amount requested. I agreed to repay in monthly installments of a set amount I thought I could manage. I was to make the repayment checks out to Eve as she was the one who now handled the household accounts.

I returned home with check in hand feeling relieved to have dodged that bullet. I continued with my daily meditation and affirmations, but my miserable symptoms did not abate. I felt a little better by Sunday night, but when I resumed my rigorous schedule on Monday, I slipped back to square one. The tax bill was paid off by mid-April and the dismal days of winter were done. The glorious weather arrived. The "golden" hills of California turned a lush green, and the flowering pear trees were in full bloom. There was no more wonderful place weather-wise to be living than in a Mediterranean climate in the spring. It lifted my spirits, but not my pain, and I eagerly anticipated closing the school year and taking summer vacation.

The end of the school term was finally approaching. I was delighted when I arrived at school, and there was an announcement posted that we were having an assembly that day. Any kind of a respite during the last few weeks of school was a welcome relief for both students and teachers. Since I had both a primary and upper grade combination class, I could choose to attend either the morning or afternoon assembly scheduled for the day. Our school did not have an auditorium, so we had to split the student body in half and fit about three hundred children into a good-sized central pod area used as a learning center for the upper grade classrooms that surrounded it.

I decided to attend the first assembly with the primary grades, which would afford me a quick break while my class was being supervised by the other teachers. The presenter was a professional magician. He had all the required paraphernalia: his cute little scantily clad female assistant, his jet-black tux with top hat and magic wand, the requisite white rabbit, along with two beautiful doves. The children were seated cross-legged on the floor with a space for the performers in an area that had been kept clear for them at the front of the room. All the teachers and a few staff members were seated on folding chairs placed along the back of the room.

The magician began his performance with the animals. The rabbit was extracted from the top hat, handed to the assistant, and deposited back into its cage. The doves were sent through their paces with delighted exclamations from the young audience. At the end of this part of his act, the magician put one dove on each of his gloved forefingers and threw both birds simultaneously up in the air. One of birds fluttered obediently into its cage at the magician's feet. My heart went out to the dear animal for spending a life in captivity for our entertainment.

Much to everyone's surprise, however, the second bird flew out over the room. As the children's eyes followed the errant dove, it sailed directly to the back wall of the room, banked around in my direction, then landed on my head! I sat stunned at the feeling of a bird's claws in my hair as it settled down to roost—and there it sat. Lest I startle the poor creature, I put my forefinger up close to it, hoping it would choose the offered perch, not my head. The children stared with wide-eyed amazement, and some squealed with delight to see Mrs. Odom with a bird nesting on the top of her head. The magician's helper struggled to make her way through the mass of excited children to come to my rescue.

If this was part of the act, it was a good thing I love birds. Most people would be in a panic about having a bird in their hair.

My thought was interrupted by the female assistant, who stood before me in her strapless sequined costume, offering profuse apologies as she lifted the dove from my head. But the show must go on, so everyone turned their attention back to enjoy the rest of the performance. Soon I was back in the classroom dismissing the children for lunch. As I passed through the learning center on my way to the faculty lunch room, the magician was still there getting ready for the afternoon performance.

"Aren't you the teacher who sat so still when Toby decided to take his

*Health is inner peace.*
*Therefore, healing is letting go of fear.*
*To make changing the body our goal is to fail to recognize*
*that our single goal is peace of mind.*

—*A Course in Miracles*

*Part II*

# CHRISTMAS 1986 TO FALL 1987

*Seven*

# QUEST

Nothing much changed with my physical symptoms, but a subtle shift had taken place inside me since I was anointed with a peaceful mind. Out of the three hundred or more heads in that room, I did not for one minute believe it was a random accident that Toby the dove landed on my head. Now I was determined to focus on making peace with my monkey mind and neutralizing the fear to get my body back to full health. Since the contracts issued by the district had already been signed for the next school term, I contacted Shirley and we made arrangements with our site administrator and the district office to job-share. Both of us would be in the classroom together the first and last two weeks of the school year, but would alternate one week on and one week off for the period in between. The schedule sounded heavenly, but the thought of reducing my income to half salary was terrifying.

My second step was to inform Ed he would have to find a replacement for me to supervise the Our House program. He was kind enough to let me know that was going to be a tall order and how much he and the whole community appreciated the program I created.

My parting shot was, "Thank you so much for the compliment, Ed. Our House will be an even better program when you recruit senior volunteers and lobby to pay the site supervisors a high enough salary to incentivize them to stay in their position for the whole year."

With the entire summer before me, I cast about for more information on healing. Back in the mid-eighties this was not as simple as going online and putting in the right search words. During this era, information was disseminated either through books, by word of mouth, or in an academic setting. However, I reasoned if little Bainbridge Island in provincial Washington State could have a shop containing a metaphysical book selection with volumes on self-healing, then surely I could find something similar in the San Francisco Bay Area. So, at my very next meeting, I checked in with Loren to see if she could steer me to community resources that might help me regain my health since the medical system had nothing to offer me. Again, she told me to stick around after group and she would have some suggestions.

"The first place you might want to check out, Carolyn, is a church group called Unity of Walnut Creek." She handed me a six-page newsletter titled "Centerpoint" as she continued. "They have a nice little bookstore with a wide variety of books you may find helpful. They also offer events and workshops of all kinds, so you could meet and interact with others looking for a better way of being in the world."

The word church set off internal alarm bells. "Is it like a religious cult?" I asked cautiously.

"No, the Unity principles were developed for people who consider themselves spiritual, but not religious. They embrace the common truths of all the world's major religions, but try to avoid the dogma." Then Loren added in sort of an off-hand way, "Carolyn, what do you know about channeling?"

"About what?" It sounded like a nautical term to me, but I hadn't a clue about what it was.

"Well, there's a book I recommend you read. It's called *Out on a Limb* and it's written by the actress Shirley MacLaine. When you finish with it, let me know and I have another resource here in the area you might be interested to know about."

Armed with resources and the promise of more, I set about deciding where to get started. I found the recommended book at B. Dalton's and then perused the Centerpoint Newsletter. The new classes had just been announced, and I selected two that really appealed to me. The first was *A Course in Miracles* study group facilitated by a former Catholic nun turned mystic. Mary was a lovely woman in her fifties, who was in the process of completing her course work at John F. Kennedy University in transpersonal psychology. My thought was that maybe I could move beyond peace of mind by studying the other six principles with Mary's guidance and the support of a spiritual community.

My second course selection was a workshop on dream analysis. This topic had always intrigued me since I had such a vivid dream life. I was fascinated with the idea of learning how to find meaning in the crazy variety of characters and events that paraded through my mind as I slumbered. As a result of the instructor's urging, I began keeping a dream journal, faithfully recording any of the dreams I could remember, even if I awakened in the middle of the night. I didn't write down every detail, but I always noted important symbols and the feeling and resulting emotions the dream evoked. Often I fell back into deep sleep and continued the same dream. I also began to notice that some of my more emotionally disturbing dreams contained some aspect of what I had been watching on television right before I went to bed. Usually, I ended my evening by watching all the tragic events from around the world being reported on the ten o'clock news.

In class I learned we dream from our subconscious mind—the part of consciousness that, more often than not, drives our behavior and forms subconscious beliefs. I was later to read that scientists believe our subconscious is very literal. It interprets everything our senses perceive from the outside environment as literal, personal, and current. My life right now was tragic and painful enough. I did *not* have to take on global suffering as well. As a result of these insights, I got rid of my TV and cancelled my subscription to the *Contra Costa Times*. I found reading carefully selected books and periodicals to be a much better way to spend my time and fill my subconscious. (That resolve continued until 2009, when I decided I wanted a television set to watch the inauguration of our first African American president.)

The Shirley MacLaine book Loren recommended was fascinating. The book was about an encounter the author has with trance channel Kevin Ryerson, which leads her to all kinds of wild and mysterious adventures at home and abroad. I knew *A Course in Miracles* was scribed by a woman who received transmissions that she "heard" in her head. That seemed strange enough, but trance channels went one step further into weird. These individuals actually put themselves into an altered state and allowed some disembodied entity to take possession of their thoughts and vocal chords to transmit information and answer questions for whomever is present in the room where the "channeling" is being conducted. A lot of times questions were asked and answers given that were of a personal nature after the channel's introductory remarks.

When I returned to group and let Loren know I had completed the book and was very interested in additional resources, she gave me the phone number of a woman who hosted a trance channel twice a month in her home. I made arrangements to attend the very next event. The channel's name was Lin Martin and he was accompanied by his wife, Stacey. In his brief introduction to open the meeting, Lin shared with the group that he had gone to the same "spook school" as Kevin Ryerson, the trance channel who became famous with MacLaine's book. The entity that spoke through Lin simply called itself Teacher. I was to learn that this disembodied intelligence was coming not from one disincarnate being, but from a collective of entities in another dimension of reality. Teacher was a collective that was particularly focused on healing—healing not just the physical body, but humanity as a whole.

After Lin went into trance and Teacher began to speak through him, the first comment concerned truth. The group was told there are many different paths and truths to enlightenment, but we must discern for ourselves our own unique journey. We were told to go within and ask, "Does this information resonate with me?" then follow the guidance we received. This guidance could be given in many different forms, but with practice we would soon be able to discern our path to wholeness.

I could see how Teacher got its entity name. As a teacher myself, I had learned many years before that my job as an educator was to help my students remember what they already know. It is a process of simply helping developing minds to put experience together and apply it to new situations. If I was being admonished to "follow my guidance," then receiving information from an unknown source did not feel so mysterious and threatening. It was mine to choose, not something I had to embrace as absolute. It was a promising and empowering message.

When I had an opportunity to eventually ask "Teacher" a personal question, my inquiry was predictably about my physical symptoms, and especially the challenge I was having with knowing what to eat so my intestines wouldn't spasm and shut down. Currently, I was reduced to eating rice and carrots. I was getting pretty bored with it and was continuing to lose weight. Something known as bodywork was suggested and then came the cryptic remark that they (meaning my guides and helpers), were going to "get my feet healed up." Neither of these remarks were particularly helpful, since I had no context to give the information meaning. What was bodywork and what did it mean to get my feet healed up? I approached Lin after he came out of trance and was copying cassette tapes of the session to give to each of us to take home. Translated, bodywork meant things like massage and getting my feet healed up referred to a need to get back to nature—to connect and ground myself to the earth.

Well, the bodywork would take further investigation, but getting myself into nature was easy and free. There were lovely hills and walking trails not too far from my apartment. Beyond the hills stood Mount Diablo, the highest peak in the Coast Range of California. The Native Americans of the area had named it the devil mountain because legend spoke of how it was created from the place of fire below the earth. The geology of the area has confirmed the veracity of the legend. The Coast Range was formed by fissures developed in the earth's crust by the Ring of Fire circling the Pacific basin.

I began exploring the nearby trails and found a secluded area on the top of one of the foothills of the mountain, where I had a panoramic view of the valley below. I brought my journal and sometimes a book and even lunch or a light snack to my sacred spot under a magnificent valley oak. The cows and I spent quiet afternoons just being in and with nature. I always felt renewed afterward.

One morning I got into my car, which was parked in the carport that held the vehicles for the tenants in my building. I spied a note under my windshield wiper on the driver's side. I retrieved, opened, and read the message:

"I am a neighbor of yours in Building 6. I notice you from time to time doing your laundry. I'd like to call you sometime." It was signed, "The green car parked in the carport right behind you."

Well, that was strange. I was now being propositioned by a green car. I turned and looked behind me. The spot in the carport for Building 6 directly behind me was empty—no green car in sight. I hadn't noticed anyone lately ogling me on my way to the laundry room either, but I was pretty focused on other matters.

I slipped the note into my purse, backed out of my parking space, and drove to the doctor's office for my scheduled appointment. Not too many days before, I'd detected a lump at about six o'clock on my left breast. I was not terribly concerned, because this had happened to me a couple of times before. Previously, these lumps had always checked out as a soft cyst that was easily aspirated with a simple office procedure. Because of my change in health providers, I had to select a new gynecologist from a list provided by my HMO. After doing the meet and greet thing, this doctor aspirated the lump as usual in his office, but he wanted me to return in a couple of weeks to make sure the matter was resolved. This was new, but I went ahead and scheduled the follow-up appointment before I left his office.

When I got back to the apartment, I just happened to check out the parking space in the carport directly behind my car. Sure enough, there was a very large green car, a Chrysler Imperial, parked there. It was an older model but very well kept.

*Could it be this easy? Just by doing my laundry, was a desire being fulfilled? First I find an auspicious book, and now it appears I've found someone who might be interesting to get to know. However, he could turn out to be a stalker. I will proceed more cautiously this time. I'm not about to leave my phone number.*

I went upstairs and wrote a note asking the green car to please leave its phone number, so I could call and we could just talk. I took it back downstairs and placed it under the windshield wiper on the driver's side of the big green car. Predictably, a note was under my windshield wiper the next morning with a phone number on it. I didn't call. I was much too apprehensive at the prospect of getting involved now that I was "a fallen woman." If he was wonderful, how would I possibly explain why I couldn't be intimate with him? No good could come from this. So I put the note aside and picked up my book.

Curiosity finally got the better of me, and I did call the number a few days later. His name was Wally and he was an accountant for Chevron Oil at their headquarters in Concord. He had lived in the Camelback Apartments for many years and was an avid golfer. I told him I enjoyed playing golf as well, but was quite rusty since I hadn't touched a golf club for almost two years. Sight unseen, I agreed to go golfing with him that weekend. After digging around in my storage to retrieve my long-forgotten clubs, I met Wally early Saturday morning at the appointed time. Next to his big green car stood what my mom used to call "a tall drink of water," and every inch an accountant, horn-rimmed glasses and all. We drove quite a distance to the Central Valley town of Hollister, so we had plenty of time to talk and exchange data. Definitely not a stalker, he even opened car doors for me. It was a lovely day, and I was glad I'd chanced making a new friend.

My follow-up appointment with the gynecologist came all too soon, and he examined the area where the cyst had been aspirated two weeks before. Even though I was unable to detect any kind of irregularity after the procedure, my new doctor was still concerned and thought he could detect something suspicious. He wanted me to have a biopsy performed on the area to be sure the matter was resolved. I thanked him for this dubious recommendation and said I'd let him know if I decided to schedule this more invasive procedure. I left the office feeling confused and distressed. On top of everything, now this.

I decided I wanted a second opinion, so I scanned through my physician directory and selected another gynecologist, called, and made an appointment. I told this doctor initially that I was there for a routine breast examination. I did not mention my previous encounter and the resulting recommendation. This second doctor examined me thoroughly and gave me a "clean bill of health."

"Well, I'm glad to hear that, Doctor," I said, "because I just had a colleague of yours recommend a breast biopsy be performed on what he is calling a suspicious area in my left breast. I can't feel anything, so I'm actually here for a second opinion."

"Show me the location of the area of concern? I'd like to examine that it again."

I showed him where the aspiration had been performed, and he checked me out again. When he finished, he told me to get dressed and his assistant would show me to his office down the hall. When I got to his office, he sat me down and gave me the typical line: "If you were my wife or my mother, I would recommend the biopsy just to be on the safe side."

Crap! That scared me. I'd watched my mother waste away and die from cancer. Now I was possibly facing the same fate. Wasn't early detection the best hope for a good outcome when it came to cancer? If I did nothing, by the time I had full-blown symptoms it might be too late. So, reluctantly, I called my first doctor and scheduled the surgery.

My apartment was only a few blocks from the hospital where the procedure would take place, so I decided to walk there and made arrangements with one of my sons to pick me up afterward as I was not to drive after the surgery. I don't think I have ever felt so lonely as I did on my solitary journey the few blocks to John Muir Hospital. The surgery was scheduled for early morning, so it was cold and windy as I walked up the hill to my destination.

I was shown to a room where a number of people were also preparing for surgery. We each had our own little curtained-off area with an examining table to sit on and nothing else. I was all ready to go, when the nurse pulled back the curtain and told me that my surgeon was delayed and it would be about forty-five minutes before I would be taken into the operating room. With absolutely nothing better to do than worry, I decided to meditate even though I didn't have my tape player. I took my three deep breaths and began to focus on counting backward, imagining a thirty-second digital clock like you would see in a gymnasium. If I lost the count because of a worry thought, as soon as I caught myself I'd start back at thirty and begin the count again. Before long, my mind stilled and I began to feel peaceful instead of anxious and agitated. Occasionally, I'd lose count, but there was no thought, just bliss. It was awesome.

All of a sudden, the curtain was jerked open and there was my nurse. "I'm sorry if I startled you," she apologized as she slapped a blood pressure cuff on my arm and started pumping.

"Were you meditating?"

"Yes. You didn't give me many other viable options."

"Wow," she responded. "I'm going to have to start meditating. I've never seen anyone about to go into surgery with a blood pressure this good."

I wish I could say my blissful state continued throughout the procedure. I do not remember having any kind of a pre-op consultation with my surgeon, but I do remember feeling horrified by what happened to me on that operating table to obtain a small sample of tissue to biopsy. Local anesthesia was used to numb my breast, so I was fully awake during the procedure. There was a lot of tugging and pulling. I liken it to a slab of meat on a table being sliced and mutilated. Unbeknownst to me, the doctor had made the incision clear up on the left side of my areola then pulled the skin back to access the area at six o'clock clear down at the crease under my breast. I assumed the incision would be made at the crease close to the suspicious area in question.

On my post-op visit, I asked the surgeon why he had made the incision so far away from the place to be biopsied. I was stunned by his reply.

"We go in at the edge of the nipple for cosmetic reasons. That way the scar is not so noticeable."

"Noticeable to whom? Who is going to see a scar at the crease under my breast?"

It took years for me to regain sensation in that breast. What is a little scar that may or may not show compared to the pleasure a woman derives from "the girls" being stimulated during love-making? I can only surmise that since medicine was pretty well dominated by men back in the '80s, if this was standard protocol, it was strictly for the pleasure of men and their fascination with that part of a woman's anatomy. I was furious, but not at the doctor. This surgeon was simply following standard medical practice. I was furious with myself. The biopsy came back negative as I knew it would. Why did I second guess myself and go ahead with the surgery? Once again, medicine had failed me, and I vowed to do a better job at listening to and then obeying my own inner guidance.

Summer was at an end, and the new school term was fast approaching. I was spending time at school consolidating my classroom so Shirley and I could fit all our years of accumulated materials into a single room. One evening, I received an unexpected phone call from my stepmother. My father was dead. I turned ice cold, then managed to ask her what had happened. Evidently the resection had given way, and he died of a perforated colon causing peritonitis and massive infection the doctors had been unable to control.

Stunned, my immediate question was, "Eve, why didn't you call me? He must have been in the hospital for some time."

"Well, dear, your father didn't want me to bother you kids."

I was furious and grief stricken! I didn't believe her explanation for a minute, but I thanked her for letting me know and hung up the phone. I can't begin to describe what I went through imagining my father's last days in pain and no close family around to comfort him. Tom was in Colorado, Barney in South Carolina, and me in California. We abandoned him to a new family that had great loyalties to one another, but not to us. The next blow was the news that Dad had willed his whole estate to Eve to use (or abuse) until her death. Then, if there was anything left, the three of us would split equally what remained. Eve was a very active woman—what my Aunt Care referred to as "a goer and a doer." She was not about to leave the planet any time soon.

Slowly, the brutal truth dawned upon me—Plan C had unexpectedly dissolved, and now I was strictly on my own.

*Initially, my grief didn't fit life.*
*My quest for healing began with the question,*
*"Where now do I fit?"*
*Out of that question came,*
*"Now that everything is gone, what's left?"*
*And, "Who am I? How did I get here?*
*Where do I go when I don't even think I can go on?"*

—*Benjamin Allen*

*Eight*

# DARK NIGHT

Eighteen short months had passed and all the structures I'd worked so hard to build throughout my lifetime had crumbled. From the time of my youth, I was told: "If you work hard, Carolyn, and do the right thing, you will be rewarded with a happy life." Where did I go wrong? I'd acquired a home, husband, and children, friends and family, good health, and now all that was gone. I still had my career, but it was not the creative and exciting challenge it used to be. I was reduced to dragging myself through each day in the classroom, counting the hours until my next week off, so I could rest and recover.

Each month when it came time to pay my bills, I wrote a check to Eve, for repayment of the loan I had taken from my father, with rage and resentment boiling up from my gut. It did not escape my notice that was the exact area where I was experiencing the greatest pain.

*She knows I'm struggling. Now that Dad's gone and she has all his money, the least she could do would be to forgive the rest of the loan. I've already paid back most of it.*

It was at this point that I started asking all the existential questions: Who am I? What is my purpose? Is there a deeper meaning or are we given this life just to suffer and die? And my biggest question of all was: Do I really want to start life all over again? I was not about to jump off a bridge, but I did sink into a great dark pit of depression. Pulling my

Aunt Care's gift from the bookshelf, I turned to DEPRESSION in Louise Hay's book, *You Can Heal Your Life*. She described the spiritual meaning of depression with two words: anger and hopelessness. Yep, that fit. At her recommendation, my new affirmation became, "I now go beyond other peoples' fears and limitations. I create my own life."

But where to begin? Well, it seems mysterious forces were still at work, because I was approached by Mary, the facilitator of *A Course in Miracles* study group, to see if I might be interested in helping her fulfill the required training hours to complete the internship requirement for her counseling degree. I thought highly of Mary and was delighted that I would benefit from her mature wisdom and spirituality without having to pay any more than the cost of the room for our sessions. I knew I was still struggling with grief over the death of my father and all the other losses I'd endured recently. I was also aware of a deep anger seething under the surface of my numb exterior facade. Most of that anger was directed toward myself for ruining my life.

I don't remember many of the details of our sessions together, but I do remember the feeling. I always went away drained, but feeling much lighter. I could sense that each session was like peeling away another layer of misunderstanding about who I thought I was and the error in my thinking that had created my current situation. One of those insights was the idea that I was the girl born with the silver spoon in my mouth. I'd always been told that by family and friends. Growing up, I was the richest person I knew. Very wealthy people from Seattle had summer homes on Bainbridge Island, but the year-round residents were primarily working class families or strawberry farmers. Everybody knew my father as the community doctor, and they worked hard to pay his fees. My father's position in our small community had always been impossible for me to escape.

As a teen, all I wanted to be was one of the gang, not the girl born to wealth and privilege. What my peers no doubt judged as my aloofness, was actually my constant feelings of separation, shyness, and insecurity around others my same age. Mary helped me to understand I had been isolated because of my rheumatic heart. I did not have the normal opportunities to learn to interact with my peers during my most formative years. Mary helped me to see all of the times my emotional needs had not been met when I was a child, and I was surprised by how many there were. She recommended I engage in an emotional self-healing technique she called inner child work. She explained that time was an illusion—something we use in the third dimension of "reality" so our nervous system won't burn out from everything happening at once. She showed me how I could go back in time and re-parent my little girl who needed to hear different messages than those I'd come to believe about myself and the way the world worked.

To do this, I needed to answer one very important question first: What do I want? Now that I had *A Course in Miracles* to guide me, Mary assured me my answers were going to be quite different than the first time around. I certainly knew what I didn't want, but the canvas of my mind was blank as I strived to picture a new life for myself.

"Find a childhood photo of yourself. Just start by loving that little girl who missed her father and believed she had a wounded heart. Give her new and empowering messages and put no conditions on her perfection. Do you think you can start there?" Mary asked.

It seemed like a weird starting place, but I had no better idea at the time, so I went ahead with the work. I actually found a sepia-tone photograph of Mom, Barney, and me that was taken in a professional studio before my father deployed to Europe in 1943. As I did the re-parenting, one other memory kept emerging from time to time that seemed important, but unrelated to the inner child. At our next session, I described the incident to Mary.

"When I was about fourteen or fifteen, I remember one afternoon I was with my mom in her bedroom. I was looking out the window at the house my Aunt Care and Grandmother lived in right behind my father's shop (a.k.a. two-car garage). For some reason, I asked my mother why it was that Aunt Care had never married and left home. Without missing a beat, my mother responded, 'Oh, she was too bossy.' Mary, can you help me understand why this incident keeps coming up for me?"

"Very interesting," was Mary's response. "That's what we might call a cultural implant on an impressionable adolescent."

"Tell me more."

"Well, from what you've told me about your mother, she was quite a bit more compliant than your Aunt Care. Because of your grandfather's death during the Depression, your Aunt Care, as the oldest, was forced to assume the role of 'head of household.' She took on the more masculine role of breadwinner for your grandmother and her two younger sisters. What your mother perceived as bossy might better be described nowadays as self-actualized."

"But I thought working toward fulfilling your highest potential was a good thing," I protested, striving to understand what she'd just told me.

"Not to the impressionable young girl you were at age fourteen or fifteen. You were probably beginning to think about boys and what you needed to do to attract them. Both your mother and aunt grew up in the era of 'the woman's place is in the home,' not out in the world making ends meet. Young women now know they can choose both, but you were somewhat of a trendsetter for your generation. There were very few women doing husband, home, children, *and* a career all at the same time during the '50s and '60s."

*Good Lord. No wonder I was such a doormat during my marriage with that kind of belief planted inside my poor literal subconscious mind. 'Too bossy' in my mother's worldview was 'self-actualized' in the view of others who had awakened to another understanding of what it meant to be a woman in the second half of the twentieth century.*

I flew up to Washington to celebrate Thanksgiving with my brother and his family on Samish Island. It was wonderful to be hugged by Aunt Care even as she scolded me about being too skinny. We all reminisced about Mom and Dad, and the subject of my failed marriage and failing health was carefully avoided for the rest of the time I was there. Even though I was welcomed with open arms, I felt like the odd man out. I could not go back expecting things to be the same as before. On the trip home, I vowed to focus on the direction I wanted my life to go. How could I find meaning and purpose in the darkness that seemed to follow me?

With Christmas fast approaching, I cast about to find some place to spend the vacation that would not be too expensive, but would help fill the emptiness of my solitary state. Mike was away in the military and Richard would be spending the holidays with his fiancée's family in Fresno. I had discovered a free periodical at Unity Book Store called *Common Ground*. It was filled with interesting articles, and about half of the pages were devoted to promoting events being offered by individuals and groups interested in furthering their businesses and the burgeoning self-help movement sweeping the West Coast. I finally settled on partaking in something called a vision quest, not because I was particularly interested in Native American tradition, but because it was cheap and the dates fell within the parameters of my winter recess. To be perfectly frank, I didn't even know what a vision quest might be, but I did need a vision for my new life, so why not give this a try?

I called to register and received my instructions in the mail a few days later. The facilitators for this six-day event were Sedonia Cahill and her current partner, known to us only as Big Bird (an apt name since there was a certain resemblance between him and the *Sesame Street* character). There were five other participants and an assistant/cook in the group. Our first night was spent at a house in Sebastopol, where we participated in an opening ceremony and orientation. Right away I realized why the cost was so reasonable—we would be sleeping in sleeping bags, and for three of the six days we would be consuming only water. My first night was spent on a plank floor in a room shared by the other five questers. I didn't sleep a wink as I tossed and turned on the unforgiving surface, trying to ease my skinny body into a comfortable position. What had I gotten myself into?

Very early the next morning, we all set out in a large older-model van heading toward southern California. Since it was the end of December, the weather was awful, with high winds and sheets of rain slamming across the windshield. Big Bird was driving the van, and Sedonia was following him in her little compact Japanese import. The van began to act up, and we had to pull over in a small town off the Grapevine, a steeply graded highway through the Tejon Pass, north of LA. It would have been extra treacherous with the heavy rains. It took quite a while to get a part to fix the van, so we needed to go to Plan B. One of the participants had an aunt living in Pasadena, so we spent the second night on the floor of Aunt Jane's living room. Her rug was a little more forgiving than the previous night's hardwood floor, but there was still a lot of tossing and turning.

Bright and early the next morning, we headed east toward the Panamint Range, a short, rugged mountain range in the northern Mojave Desert, within Death Valley National Park. Once we got to the eastern side of the

Sierras, the weather cleared and the air was frigid and dry as a bone. By about lunchtime, we had reached our destination to set up a base camp for the quest. After lunch we were told to walk out away from camp and find a spot to spend our three days of "alone time." We were cautioned not to choose any kind of a low point, or "wash," to set up our camp. Sedonia explained that rain could collect in the nearby mountain range and cause flash flooding where we would be sleeping in the valley below. We were to note carefully the location of our spot, so we could let those at base camp know where to find us in case something happened. I had no idea how they were going to know if I needed their help, but I was committed. My mission was a vision for the new life I would craft for myself.

I was to learn there are rules to questing. We were told that what we carried into our sacred spot was the weight of our karma, so we should pack light. I wasn't exactly sure what heavy karma might bring, but it didn't sound good. I knew it would be cold, so I wore long underwear that could double for pajamas, padded ski pants, a parka, and boots, with two pairs of socks. I carried a light sleeping bag, a tarp large enough to act as both ground cover and lean-to, a jug of water, and a journal in which to write. We had work to do, so we were not allowed any books or other diversions. We were to fashion a prayer wheel out of stones, and our last night would be spent sitting in the middle of the wheel, receiving an animal helper and a vision for our future.

After receiving my instructions, I set out to claim my spot. Being alone in nature for three days was not a particular challenge to me. I had always felt more at home in a natural setting than I did around a lot of people, especially in a metropolitan area. The solitude of my childhood had taught me I had resources I could call upon to guide and comfort me. However, I was not familiar with desert habitat, so this was uncharted territory. I followed a path away from the direction the other participants were taking. I decided that when I came to a fork in the trail, I would take nothing but left turns going out from base camp until I found a good and somewhat protected place to sleep. That way, I would be taking nothing but (the) right turns to find my way back.

I had walked for about twenty minutes following my left-turn strategy until I got to a ravine that led up to the floor of the Panamint Valley and a spectacular view of the mountain range in the distance. This was the perfect place to craft my prayer wheel, but it was much too exposed to set up my camp, so I turned and headed back. As I was navigating the steep trail, I looked to my right and spotted a shining bush with almost white foliage growing out of a ledge a little higher than the top of my head. There was a fissure in the side of the ravine that allowed me to climb up onto the ledge where the bush was growing. The ledge was just large enough to lay out my tarp and sleeping bag with room at one end to dig a pit to accommodate a campfire. I had a flashlight with me, but the days were short and at this latitude I would be in darkness for almost fifteen hours each night. That was a lot of sack time for someone sleeping on the cold hard ground, so I planned to write in my journal at night by the light of a small fire. I had brought matches, but the challenge would be finding fuel in this barren terrain.

I set out my tarp and sleeping bag, found a stick to tent my tarp, and gathered enough fuel for the first night of my quest. My water and few belongings were stashed close by. Secluded and protected from the wind, it would make the perfect spot for this next experience on my hunt for meaning and purpose. As I left to report in with Sedonia and Big Bird to let them know my location, I gave gratitude to the hearty and shining shrub that had pointed the way to my perfect spot. I was one of the first to arrive back at base camp, and my inner critic immediately shared with me that I wasn't doing it right. Shortly, however, the others began to return. It was much easier for me to describe my location. There was more instruction and ceremony before we had dinner and dispersed for our three days of solitude and fasting.

During the instruction period, Sedonia had me select a card from a special Medicine Wheel deck she had brought. At random, I selected the card of the West. I was told the gift of the west was introspection and reflection, the color is black, and the season was autumn, representing death and rebirth. Further, we were told to pay special attention to our surroundings and look for meaning in the small things all around us. We were to record our insights, images, and imaginings to share with the ceremonial circle when we completed our alone time. The three facilitators remaining at base camp would be holding sacred space for us to have meaningful visions and dreams during our quest experience. Well, like the condemned (wo)man, we ate a hearty meal, after which we were all thoroughly smudged with desert sage, then sent out to our waiting sleeping quarters.

There was no burning bush or profound vision during the three days of my alone time, but it was the perfect opportunity for me to really watch the machinations of my mind. My inner dialogue was brutal. That first night, a tremendously strong wind kicked up in the early morning hours, and I thought I could hear thunder in the direction of the distant mountains. A flash flood was going to sweep out of the mountains, rush through the valley floor, and tumble down the ravine where I was sleeping. I would be swept away and nobody would find my remains. As it turned out, I was supremely warm and comfortable all night long and slept deeply for the first time in days.

My totem animal ended up being Grasshopper. I had a visitation on the third day of my quest from a very cold and sluggish trooper of the grasshopper ranks who had decided not to go underground for the winter. In Native American Indian tradition, "Grasshopper leaps into your midst from out of nowhere. It carries the high vibration of the mystical beauty of a free spirit; free to do and go as it pleases with no knowing what the next move will be. Grasshopper invites us to dance with imagination so we can practice quiet observation that reveals the multiple choices of our future. With each choice we make, new dimensions open up to us. Grasshopper energy is an ongoing dance of the balance of having your feet on the ground and in tune with the cycles of the earth while your thoughts are in fanciful flight of daydreams. Grasshopper encourages you to dream and to put your dreams into action."

A free spirit was the last thing I had thought for myself. Grasshopper, bring it on! I was captured by the collective beliefs of my culture and had obediently followed all its dictates, so the place of mystery was where I was being guided. Could I dare to go beyond the established convention and strike out into unexplored territory? It was a terrifying and empowering question.

My last night spent in the Medicine Wheel was filled with contemplating this kind of question. The instructions were that we enter the wheel at sunset and sit in prayer and contemplation until sunrise. This was my last day without food, and I gave deep gratitude for the give-away creatures—the plants and animals that gave me sustenance throughout my lifetime. This was the first time in my life I had ever gone a whole day, let alone three days, without food. The second day was tough because of the headache, but the last day was bliss. My monkey mind quieted, and it felt as though I was pulling energy from the things of nature—the sun, the pure water I drank, and the throbbing rhythmic emissions from Mother Earth. Hereafter, I vowed I would go to the natural environment to revitalize and recover from the craziness of the "civilized" world.

When I returned to base camp, I was told that one of the participants had been unable to complete her alone time and had been taken to a nearby hospital. Evidently, the facilitators' precautions were warranted even though I had discounted their safety measures as drama. Nothing had been threatening about my experience except my own inner demons. Maybe I *was* moving into a more empowered way of being.

After sharing our experience of sacred time, I was given my Native American name: Looks Within. Sedonia had given me the perfect name to help me see the depression I was dealing with was my body saying I was too outer directed. It was time to go within myself for the answers I had been seeking. I could still use others to help me re-member what I already knew, but I had to begin to trust and act upon my own inner guidance.

It did not escape my notice that right after my vision quest ordeal, I came away feeling better than I had in many months. My bowels were functioning on a regular basis, and the constant pain in my gut diminished. I wish I could say this was a lasting state. I was back now, however, in the world of the two-leggeds; back to the stark reality of survival in the work-a-day world. It was the month of February and the middle of seven years of drought in California. This scourge had depleted the fluid from Mother Earth's veins and withered the landscape as far as the eyes could see.

This bleak winter scene matched my developing mood, for I felt stripped and devoid of life force and was struggling to complete my teaching contract for the term.

*If only I can get my body to work properly again, then all will be well and the pain will go away. I can recover my energy and move with power and confidence, this time by myself, strong and autonomous. If only this unrelenting pain in my gut would leave, then I can let go of the fear in my heart that something is wrong, terribly and irreversibly wrong with me.*

Casting about for relief, I remembered the important realization I'd had on my vision quest. Upon reaching forty, I'd declared to friends and family that no longer would I submit to the discomforts and indignities of camping and being outdoors in nature. Now that I had achieved middle-age status, I had earned the right to travel in style and stay in luxury hotels. What a joke! It had been dramatically demonstrated to me on my quest how much I needed contact with the earth in order to ground, center, and restore balance to my troubled body, emotions, and spirit.

I had survived beautifully for three days in the desert, during the dead of winter, totally alone and without food. One Saturday that February, after a particularly difficult week at school, it occurred to me, if I could just lay my belly once again on the ground, I would feel better. A second-floor apartment was not too conducive to communing with nature, so I impulsively decided to spend the night on the mountain.

I quickly packed my tarp and sleeping bag in my backpack along with some water, a book, and a votive candle, which I had discovered to be an adequate light source for reading after dark. I parked at the end of the deserted cul-de-sac near the trailhead for Regency Gate and began the climb up the north peak of Mount Diablo.

The day was clear, cold, and dry. I followed the now-empty streambed for about two-and-a-half miles, my toxic body aching and head pounding. I knew this trail well, but never thought of the possibility of camping here. Easing my load from my back, I looked about for a place to stay. This area seemed much too exposed although I was fairly sure no one would be out on the trails this time of year. I hefted my pack to my back once again and continued my climb up toward my beloved waterfall, which I knew was now totally dry. After another half mile, I came to a turn in the trail that seemed important. Moving a few hundred feet off the trail, I found a secluded area with a high embankment on one side and a steep cliff covered with chaparral on the other. The two features narrowed into a small animal trail leading around the outcropping of the bank.

This was perfect! No one could see me here, even if I started a small fire, which I fully intended to do. I arranged one side of the tarp on the ground as a ground cover, found a sturdy stick to prop the remaining half of the tarp up at one end to form a tent, then placed my sleeping bag, candle, and book in place to prepare for the night.

With my shelter in place, I gathered wood and started a small fire just as the sun slipped behind the horizon. As I gazed into the dancing flames, I began to reflect upon how solitary my life had become since my children had grown and I had left my marriage. I was alone in the world, and this evening's odyssey brought that fact more clearly into focus than ever before. Here I was in the dark, high on a mountain, with a more than two-hour hike between me and the car, and nobody even knew or cared where I was.

Laughing at myself, the suburban camper, I lit my candle and crawled into my sleeping bag to read my book, *The Mists of Avalon*. Now, if one really wanted adventure, I mused, all one really had to do was submerge oneself into the depths of Arthurian legend. Eventually the fire dwindled, then the candle sputtered and went out. I curled up in my warm bag and fell into a deep sleep.

Did I dream? I didn't think so. I was wrenched suddenly awake by a blood-chilling scream as the quiet of deep morning was split in two. What on earth? I flattened myself to the ground and again the roar—this time closer and identifiable as a very angry mountain lion, not much further than about twenty feet behind my flimsy shelter.

Sheer terror gripped me as I stared wide-eyed into the cold blackness, casting about for a plan. To run was impossible in this darkness. I had no light and my only weapon was the stick, somewhere near my hand, that tented my tarp. What a fool I was to have come up here alone with no protection. I would be mauled and eaten, and no one would even know where to look for my remains. I waited, huddled in my sleeping bag, for the claws of the cat to slash through the tarp.

In the deafening silence that followed, a certain calm began to settle about me, and I gently surrendered to the understanding there was no escape, at least not on a physical level. If I were to transmute this situation, I must change my emotional state. Animals could sense fear, and fear meant prey.

*After all, here I am the interloper on this creature's territory. She is angry and rightfully so. Can I follow the teachings of The Course? Can I choose love instead of fear?*

Slowly I willed myself to become peaceful. I then began to dialogue in my mind, sending loving and compassionate thoughts out across the darkness to my mighty teacher. The communication continued for many long minutes. These minutes eventually turned into an hour, and at last I fell once again into a deep and uninterrupted sleep until awakened by the first light of dawn.

*Wounds don't heal the way you want them to,*
*they heal the way they need to.*
*It takes time for wounds to fade into scars.*
*It takes time for the process of healing to take place.*
*Give yourself that time. Give yourself that grace.*
*Be gentle with your wounds. Be gentle with your heart.*

*—Dele Olanubi*

*Nine*

# LETTING GO

My recent encounters with the animal world—Dove of Peace, Grasshopper, and now Cougar—were too weird to be coincidental. They demonstrated for me that there is another level of reality that exists apart from how *I* thought the world worked. This other level was the place of the miraculous. However, it was ephemeral. I wanted to know how to slip into this empowered place more consistently.

A visit from Cougar, according to *Spirit Animal Totems,* was to be taken as: "a sign that you have come into your own power. It's time for you to take charge of the situation and be strong. Cougar can also signify that you should leap into all of the opportunities that are being offered to you right now. Use the power of your intentions and be clear with where you are going. Cougar also asks us to balance our power. Learn to know when gentleness is needed and when asserting your energy will bring you your goal. Above all Cougar teaches us how to use our leadership qualities without ego."

Apparently, I possessed an internal knowing, an intelligence that had a great desire for my ego-self, or persona, to grow and change. *A Course in Miracles* refers to the ego as "the false-self." My meditation practice had given me a real up-close and personal look at my ego—that monkey mind that screamed at me continually to blame others, to judge and fear more, do more, be more and have more. Meditation training was the practice of simply noticing this chatter, then letting the thought go and returning to a point of focus. I was learning to become the observer of my thoughts, rather than constantly feeling the emotion that those negative thoughts evoked. It was almost like there was two of me: the egoic me that constantly dredged up painful events from my past only to project them out into the future in the form of worry and fear; and the spiritual me that observed myself thinking those thoughts, then simply letting them go.

I had arrived at that scary place of perceptual meaninglessness—a state of ignorance—where things lost the meaning I had given them through my cultural conditioning. The idea that I didn't understand anything was my challenge as the winter of 1987 passed into another dry spring. My sessions with Mary continued to reveal how the meanings I had drawn from earlier life experiences led to faulty thinking. According to Mary, meanings, when given by the ego, are not absolutes. *A Course in Miracles* goes so far as to call them false assumptions. Mary encouraged me to begin doing the lessons in the teacher's workbook for *The Course*. Evidently, the text was providing me a theoretical framework for the teachings, but doing the lessons in the workbook makes the goal of *The Course* attainable. These lessons were a way to change my worldview. They would teach me how to see my life with new eyes. To accomplish this would require retraining my mind with new beliefs. In fact a direct quote from *The Course* states: "Miracles occur naturally as expressions of love. The real miracle is the love that inspires them. In this sense, everything that comes from love is a miracle." My current beliefs appeared to be making me sick. It was time for an overhaul.

So I tackled the lessons, vowing to do one each day until I completed all 365 of them. Just to give you an example of my challenge, here are the first four lessons: "1) Nothing I see in this room [on this street, from this window, in this place] means anything; 2) I have given everything I see in this room [on this street, from this window, in this place] all the meaning that it has for me; 3) I do not understand anything I see in this room [on this street, from this window, in this place]; 4) These thoughts do not mean anything. They are like the things I see in this room [on this street, from this window, in this place]."

I was definitely in trouble from that first lesson. The obvious and terrifying conclusion, if the first four lessons were correct, was "I know nothing!" How does one function if this was the natural order of things? After all, I made a career out of teaching children what I thought I knew about the material world and how things worked. Now I was being guided to let go of these perceptions. Everything my sensory organs were telling me about my world did not actually exist. What always seemed solid and absolutely real was actually more like a simulation—a projected hologram that could be made to collapse if I would start to "see" my world with new eyes. To see with spiritual eyes requires us to let go of crediting meaning to the world that we see with physical eyes. From this perspective, neutrality becomes the path to freedom and peace of mind—repeating the phrase, "nothing is right, wrong, good, or bad." It is simply what is happening in the moment. I even began to think of my spiritual vision as the inward eye or eyes of my heart.

My next challenge was to understand love in a different way. The English language is very limited in its ability to differentiate between romantic love as something we do, and love as a state of being. If we love our husband, it is the verb form of the word since we are performing an action. If we are being love, the word's function becomes a noun. When *The Course* speaks of love, it is not referring to the action of giving and receiving; instead, it is naming the essence of our state of being. The "Introduction" clearly states *The Course* does not "aim at teaching the meaning of love, for that is beyond what can be taught." It does work to remove the blocks to our awareness of love's presence. In the ordinary world, the opposite of love is fear, but what is "all encompassing," according to *The Course,* can have no opposite.

So, here I was at paradox. The *Oxford Dictionary* defines paradox as "a self-contradictory, essentially absurd statement, a person or thing conflicting with preconceived notions of what is reasonable or possible." As Alice in Wonderland said after falling down the rabbit hole, things were getting "curiouser and curiouser" in my world. This reality I was trying to understand followed very different rules than the ones I had played by for most of my life. My body, however, was simply too uncomfortable for me *not* to explore this other world. Finally, I concluded that if I could not intellectually understand it, I could at least learn to "stand in the mystery" of it and proceed with my life.

*Ten*

# MOVING ON

My resolve to view my world with new eyes led me to my next step on the journey of self-discovery. One evening, I was attending another session with trance channel Lin Martin. At the conclusion of Teacher's encouraging message, Lin announced that he and Stacey were conducting a conference in late June that he referred to as an integration training to be held in Denmark. It would include instruction in bodywork and "other ways of knowing" through extra-sensory perception (ESP). The event included a three-day float trip through the waterways of the Danish Jutland. This opportunity presented itself shortly after I learned Lee had finally sold the house, and I would be receiving my half of the equity as soon as the escrow closed in the next few weeks.

Since childhood, one of my favorite things to peruse was the *National Geographic* magazine. Those glossy images of exotic people and places implanted within me a deep desire to travel, but I married young. Most of my adult life was occupied with bending to Lee's idea of travel. He did not have an adventurous bone in his body and would only go to places where he would be meeting friends, usually his bar buddies, who had summer residences within the western United States. Finally, here was my opportunity to get out and see the world, whether I was in pain or not. Wasn't my visit from Cougar indicating that "I should leap into all the opportunities being offered to me right now?" Well, I was being offered the opportunity of a lifetime, and I jumped at the chance.

I had a lot to accomplish in preparation for such a trip. Since I had never stepped foot out of the US, I needed to get a passport for the first time in my life and a Eurail Pass to explore Europe after the conference. Since the pass was not valid in England, I also acquired an international driver's license, so I could rent a car in England to make my way to Heathrow Airport for my return trip. Stacey gave me contact information for Doris, one of the attendees who was looking for someone to share expenses for a rental car so we could get to the Danish town of Viborg, where the conference was being held. We made arrangements to fly into Hamburg, Germany, rent a car, and drive to our destination. Doris had been an airline hostess when she was younger, so I was relieved to know my companion was a seasoned traveler.

I almost missed my flight. Never having flown internationally, I did not know the distinction between boarding and departure flight time. Wally drove me to San Francisco International, and we were enjoying a leisurely breakfast at the airport while waiting for my fight. As I was strolling toward the gate about twenty minutes before my flight time, my name was announced over the loudspeaker to report to the boarding area immediately. I was the last one to be hurried onto the plane right before the doors closed and the jet taxied into position on the runway.

"Where have you been?" Doris asked as I collapsed into the seat next to her.

Embarrassed to admit I'd been lollygagging with my boyfriend, I mumbled something about getting stuck in traffic as I settled myself and struggled with my seat belt. I stuck to Doris like glue during the layover and transfer at Kennedy International. Soon I was wending my way across the Atlantic on one of the most humongous jets I had ever seen. Our seating was toward the rear of the plane, only one row ahead of the smoking section. The offensive smoke continually drifting over from the seat directly behind me started to give me a headache. I finally got smart and directed the overhead air vent full blast toward the chain-smoker to my rear. About a half hour later, I felt a tap on my shoulder.

"Would you turn off that air blowing on me? It's giving me a sore throat," complained my fellow traveler.

"Did you ever consider the irritating effects of chain-smoking on the tissues of your throat?" was my retort. "I was just providing both of us with a little fresh air."

Where had that come from? Usually I would have apologized and meekly complied with a direct request like that. My motto was always: "Peace at any cost." Again, I was surprised when the disgruntled traveler mumbled something under his breath, but sat down without further comment. The stand-off led to cigarettes put away, vents off, lights out, and both of us getting some sleep. I was awakened by a general announcement from the cockpit. There had been an unexpected change in the flight plan, and we would be landing and changing planes in West Berlin before proceeding to Hamburg. Being unceremoniously dropped off behind the Iron Curtain had not been on my agenda, but if it was adventure travel I wanted, this was an auspicious beginning to my journey. (West Berlin was an island of the Western-aligned Federal German Republic, completely surrounded by Eastern German under the control of Russia. The Iron Curtain did not fall until the next year.)

Dumped would be more accurate word for it. There were no further instructions from the cockpit about connecting flights. The West Berlin airport was a madhouse. With Doris leading the way, we tried to get information on how to find the gate for our flight to Hamburg. Our attempts to communicate were lost in translation, so my experienced traveling companion found the *Auskunft* kiosk and, armed with proper directions, we wove through the terminal throng toward the designated loading area. With not much time to spare, we were ushered onto a smaller plane and deposited in Hamburg sans luggage. Our bags did not make the transfer in Berlin. Doris reassured me and sat me down to wait while she negotiated the retrieval of our bags. We had planned to stay the night in Hamburg, pick up the rental car, and begin our road trip into Denmark the following day. Both of us had a carry-on with all the necessities for overnight, so it would be simply the inconvenience of returning to the airport to pick up our errant luggage. In my case this consisted of a backpack, sleeping bag, and enough travel and camping clothes for a couple of weeks. True to my vow, I also included the teacher's workbook for *A Course in Miracles,* so I could continue the lessons.

It was a glorious motor trip from Hamburg, through northern Germany, and into Denmark straight north to Viborg. It's been thirty years, but I can still remember the rolling hills covered in green, with occasional checkerboard fields of bright yellow mustard flower. The contrast after the dingy appearance of the industrial city of Hamburg was striking. Often the neat little country homes were very close to the road—some still topped with thatched rooves. My expectation was that some little hobbit would soon emerge from the welcoming front door and wave as we passed by.

My next moment of delight was driving between the large white pillars that provided entry to a circular drive that passed in front of the structure where I would be taking up residence for the next few weeks. Hald Manor is a majestic structure, last rebuilt in the late seventeen hundreds, only twenty-two years after the signing of the Declaration of Independence here in the United States. I wondered how old some of the little houses were that I recently passed on my trip. All throughout Europe, I was continually struck by how much older and well-cared for everything was compared to buildings in the US. Neat as a pin would have been my mother's description of Denmark and its people if she'd ever had the opportunity to travel.

Upon entering the building, we were greeted by a grand entry with a magnificent staircase leading to the meeting rooms above. Ancient oil paintings of former lords and ladies of the manor in commanding poses hung on the wall up to the second and third story of the central building—a reminder of the past feudal system of Danish government. When the Harry Potter movies came out a while back, I remember thinking how much the talking portraits in the stairwell of the Hogwarts School of Witchcraft and Wizardry reminded me of the paintings hanging in Hald Manor.

My assigned roommate was Anita, a bodyworker from a small town in north central Sweden. The conference attendees were mostly Danes, Swedes, and Americans, along with four German women and one man from Holland. I was impressed by how well all the Europeans spoke

English, some with no accent whatsoever. Our first evening together, we played a game to help us remember each other's names. When selected, we were to repeat the names of those who had already introduced themselves and then give our name and share a little bit about ourselves. Well, I wasn't in the last and most challenging position in the circle of approximately thirty-five attendees, but I failed miserably making it around the circle when it came my turn to remember all those exotic European names.

Lin and Stacey had done a brilliant job organizing the event. We all took turns helping with meal preparation and cleanup. The strictly vegetarian food was delicious, but my gut was not happy with all the grains, lentils, and beans. I simply did not have the enzymes to digest this form of protein, and the resulting gas caused my bowels to shut down. I was miserable and far from home. The solution, according to Teacher, was to go swimming each morning in Hald Lake. I was assured the cold water and exercise would help to stimulate blood flow to the bowels and get things moving again.

At the back of Hald Manor, there were concrete stairs leading down to a massive lawn with a long reflection pool, centered to showcase the central building. At the far end of the pool were two pavilions once used as dressing rooms for people to change into swimsuits. Just beyond these small outbuildings was Hald Lake. Faithful to Teacher's advice, I awakened early each morning, meditated, did my lesson for the day, then slipped out of the manor and made my way down to the water's edge. Stimulating was putting it mildly. The water was not just cold—bracing and frigid would be a better description. It accomplished what I had set out to do, however. My whole body would flush with warmth once I dried off.

Each day the assembled group had new challenges presented to them. One of our first activities was learning therapeutic massage and chakra balancing. I had never had a professional massage. My belief about massage, formed during childhood, had always been that it was just an excuse to promote illicit sex. Growing up, I was cautioned to stay away from First Avenue in Seattle, because that was where all the pimps, prostitutes, tattoo shops, and massage parlors were located. Further, I had never heard the word "chakra." It seems that humans are endowed with seven invisible wheels located running up the front of the body. Since these energy vortices fall outside the realm of what the physical eye can detect, I had no idea I possessed such phenomena and was utterly clueless about imbalances in the system and how to restore it.

It seems imagination and intent are important components to the rejuvenation of these wheels. At the end of the massage, the recipient was lying on their back. We were taught a series of positions we were to perform with our hands as we acted as conduits to balance and harmonize our massage recipient's chakras. I was certainly learning to have faith in the process, because one of my psychic gifts was NOT clairvoyance. No matter how hard I tried, I could not "see" these wheels, nor could I feel any kind of change taking place before I made the leap of faith that I accomplished what was needed with one position of the hands and then move on to the next. There was plenty of rotation among partners, so we had ample opportunity to get to know each other with and without clothes. Only the four German women were a little reclusive, but I think that was because they did not speak or understand English as well as the rest of the attendees.

Although I did not particularly excel in the massage and chakra balancing, I found I had a real talent at psychometry. Psychometry is the ability to discover facts about an event or person by simply holding an object that is intimate to the person you are "reading." My partner for this practice activity was a young Swedish woman named Eva, who had lived in the States growing up, so she spoke English with no discernable accent. When we spoke with each other on kitchen duty, I had discovered she was attending this spiritual conference to have time away from her fiancé before they got married at the end of summer.

We settled ourselves on Eva's bed, and she handed me a locket she had been wearing around her neck. "This is something Viktor gave to me shortly after we started dating. I wear it a lot, so you can hold this."

"Do you have any particular question or subject you would like me to get information on, or do you just want a general reading?"

"Well, I'm really nervous about our decision to finally get married. I don't know if we should wait or go ahead with the date we've set."

I held the locket in both hands and brought my hands up to my heart. Then I shut my eyes and set the intent to get information on Eva's impending nuptials. My monkey mind, of course, started screaming at me:

*You can't do this. It's impossible to get information from a little piece of jewelry. What if I tell her something that she doesn't want to hear? What if I make up something and it's wrong? I have no right to get involved in the private life of almost a complete stranger...*

I took three deep clearing breaths, wrapped up all that ego ranting and let it float away in a pink balloon, then simply sat for a moment in blessed stillness. From that quiet place, I started to speak. I really don't recall my exact words, but the gist of the message was that a wedding would take place, but not as planned. It would be in a different place and at a different time. Most startling to both of us, however, was the last impression I shared with Eva.

"I'm also to let you know you will not be marrying Viktor." I finished the session by reassuring my partner that I had never done anything like this before and not to put too much faith in my psychic veracity.

Eva looked at me strangely, then said, "If I get real honest with myself, Carolyn, I felt a great sense of relief run all through my body when you told me Mr. Right is not Viktor. I knew when I decided to come to this event that I wasn't feeling right about the marriage. I think we set a date because that's what all our family and friends expected of us." We parted friends and Eva began to try to convince me to come stay with her in Stockholm when the conference ended instead of taking off across Europe with my rail pass.

The camping and canoe excursion through the Jutland was almost dreamlike. Paddling through the locks and along the waterways of the Danish countryside was, in itself, a meditation. We frequently sighted wild swans along with local farmers working the fields. The neat and tidy little houses reminded me of the illustrations I had enjoyed as a youngster when I read Hans Christian Andersen's fairy tales, like "The Ugly Duckling."

I had return airline tickets out of Heathrow in London, but planned to wing it by staying in youth hostels and bed and breakfast places along the way. All these plans began to change as we got closer to the end of the training and our time together. Instead of striking out on my own as planned, I got captured by Swedes. We had formed cherished friendships through our partner exchanges. It seemed I was in high demand to come visit some of the dear souls I had gotten to know so well. We all sat around a campfire the last night of our canoe expedition, and the Scandinavians planned my itinerary for the remainder of my time in Europe.

Benta was a lovely young Danish woman who did bodywork and sold crystals and other semi-precious gemstones. In fact, I still keep a tiny crystal ball on my desk that I bought from her. Benta and I drove from Hald Manor to her tidy little apartment in Copenhagen. After a few days touring that ancient capital, Benta put me on a train to Sweden with promises on both our parts to keep in touch. The train was loaded onto a large ferry to make the short crossing from Denmark to Sweden.

I continued north on the train to visit my roommate, Anita, in a small country village located in north central Sweden. I had a strong feeling of déjà vu as I traveled through the Swedish countryside. The red houses and barns trimmed in white were very similar to the Skagit Valley in the state of Washington near where I grew up. Even many of the wild flowers I examined on a hike we took were the same halfway 'round the world. No wonder so many Scandinavians settled in the Pacific Northwest. It was like coming back home. Anita was a skilled bodyworker, and under her talented hands long-held tensions were released from my back, neck, shoulders, and upper arms. It was an enchanting initiation to the magic of therapeutic massage lovingly administered.

My next stop was Stockholm, where I was supposed to meet Eva at the clock tower outside the train station. This trip occurred before cellphones, so communication was a challenge. I emerged from the station, found my way to the clock tower, and looked around for my next hostess. Eva was nowhere to be seen. Everything had gone so smoothly up to this point. Where could she be? I had spoken briefly to her from Anita's house the day before to arrange to be picked up. She knew I was coming, and told me she had something important to share and was anxious to see me. Where was she? I couldn't see her anywhere. Panic spread through me as I thought about all the worst-case scenarios. About a half hour passed before I heard the honking of a horn and there was Eva. I loaded my bags into her car while she apologized profusely for keeping me waiting.

"Oh, Carolyn. I'm so sorry to be late and so glad you're here. You won't believe what has happened to me since I left you in Viborg. I've found my soulmate. Everything you told me in the psychometry reading has come true!"

"Boy, that was quick," was my stunned reply. "Tell me more."

"Well, the whole way back from Viborg, I thought about what I was going to tell Viktor when I got home. I decided I had to find some way to let him know I didn't want to get married. When I got back I couldn't get in touch with him, but I did have a message from someone I'd known in the corporate world where I used to work. He said he was in town and wanted to take me out to dinner. We have not been apart since that dinner."

"Ah, Mr. Right, I presume. What are you going to do with me?"

"Oh, Erik had to leave this morning. That's why I'm late. He won't be back until late next week. But, needless to say, I have been a little distracted. By the way, Henrik called me this morning, and he wants to take you sightseeing and to dinner Saturday night. Are you okay with that?"

Henrik taught high school students English, and we had done psychic processes together at the training and shared a canoe on the excursion down the river. He mentioned his desire to see me when I reached Stockholm, but we had not really made any solid plans. I guess my Swedish friends had everything handled.

"Sounds wonderful. And that will give you some time to get settled. I'll call Henrik when we get to your place."

Most of my time with Eva was taken up hearing about Erik. Of all the processes I learned during the conference, psychometry was my biggest success. I may not have been able to see invisible wheels on the body, but I could hear wise messages generated from inside myself. I was later to learn that this is called clairaudience—"the ability to perceive sounds or words from outside sources in the spirit world. Psychics who are clairaudient hear voices, sounds, or music that are not audible to the normal ear. They receive these messages mentally or within their ears." I had always joked that I got my best insights from one-liners delivered by an inner voice that was blunt, but very wise. I was thrilled to know I could also get helpful information on others' behalf.

My next discovery about this inner voice was its ability to keep me safe. Henrik picked me up on Saturday about mid-afternoon and we toured museums, city buildings, and other points of interest in Stockholm. I was wearing my safari skirt, blouse, and scarf, with my camera around my neck, looking every inch the tourist. I had a large fabric carry-all over my shoulder, containing all my ID and other valuables. As we walked down a busy sidewalk, my "voice" commanded me to protect my purse and cross to the other side of the street. In one swift move, I checked for traffic as I swung my valuables to face front, then grabbed Henrik's arm.

"Let's go across the street and look at that building, so I can take a picture," I ordered.

Henrik complied, but I'm sure he wondered about my swift maneuver. So did I, until I glanced back over my shoulder and saw four scruffy youth peel off and disappear out of sight around the corner. A chill ran through my body as I lifted my camera and took a picture of a rather nondescript building. Henrik seemed so proud of his city, I didn't want to cast any kind of shadow over our lovely afternoon together. We eventually made our way down to the waterfront, and boarded a large tour boat.

We ate a delightful dinner as we cruised through the Stockholm Archipelago. The archipelago consists of 30,000 islands, islets, and skerries. Our tour took us to a skerry, one of the small rocky uninhabited islands. A band was waiting for us there on a concrete slab that also acted as a dock for our tour boat. In high summer, this area is far enough north that it is only dark for a few hours each night. We danced to the music of accordions and horns in the midnight sun. Henrik was surprised that I knew the polka and schottische. I shared with him that I'd grown up with Norwegians and Swedes, and these were some of the first dances we learned in junior high school.

Before I knew it, the time came to head toward England so I could catch my flight back to the States. Eva helped me get reservations on a ship that would take me across the North Sea to Harwich, England. My plan was to rent a car in that seaport town, so I could enjoy some time touring the heartland of my ancestors before catching my plane. I have a Dutch and an Irish grandmother, but my grandfathers were both English. So, with promises to write, Eva delivered me to the train station with tickets to Göteborg. From there I boarded what was equivalent to the poor man's cruise liner. My tiny stateroom contained four bunk beds and was shared with three other women, none of whom spoke English.

Elegant or not, this was the first time I had been on any ship larger than a ferry boat, and I was determined to make the most of my first cruise experience. I found my way up to the almost empty dining room and ordered my dinner. The weather had kicked up as soon as we left port, and the poor service staff was having a real challenge delivering my meal without it landing on the floor in the process. I ate a hearty meal and decided to find the entertainment area and enjoy the music and dancing. When I entered the ballroom, there was no band and no dancers, but there were a few passengers enjoying a drink, so I found a table and ordered a glass of wine.

I leaned over to a gentleman next to me. "Do you speak English?"

"Yes, I do and I always enjoy the opportunity to practice my English. Where are you from in America? I went to school many years ago in Michigan."

"I live near San Francisco, and I'm on my way home. What's happened to everyone? Why isn't there any music or dancing?"

My drinking partner gave me a funny look and said, "In case you haven't noticed, the sea is really rough. Most everyone is below decks getting sick. You must be one tough sailor."

When I returned some time later to my stateroom, his assessment was correct about the state of most of the passengers, including my three slightly green-looking roommates. None of us got much sleep that night as the ship rocked and rolled.

The charming little seaport town of Harwich, England was very much as I had imagined it. Growing up, we had a home library that contained the collected works of Robert Louis Stevenson and Rudyard Kipling. My childhood imagination, and Kipling's descriptions in such works as *Captains Courageous,* had portrayed a town very similar to what I was now experiencing. It was a little after lunch when I arrived, so I found a place to stay the night and got information on how to find a car rental and a good place to have dinner. The dinner recommendation was a nearby pub that closed at three, but would open again at 6:00 for dinner.

"Really, why is it closed for three hours in the afternoon?" I inquired.

"It's the law," replied my informant. "That's the only way we can get

Patty to go home after work, so his mum can grab his wages. Then she can give him a few quid to go drink at the pub with his mates if he pleases."

Well, that was quaint. So, I went for a walk on the beach to ground myself and restore my land legs. After all these years, I still have a few rocks and shells I collected on that walk. At 6:30 I entered the pub. It was smoky and dark, but the food was hearty and I was hungry. I hated to eat alone in a restaurant/bar situation, probably because Washington State had blue laws when I was growing up that would not allow a woman to get anywhere near a bar where alcohol was being served. I spotted an older gentleman sitting alone who had just been served and asked him if he minded if I joined him. I surprised myself by my boldness, but I was breaking through all my inhibitions these days, so why not give this a try. My shyness was a result of my fear of intruding upon another and being rejected. However, somewhere in my recent travels, someone had said words that made great good sense to me. The answer is always "no" if you don't ask.

Tom was delighted to welcome me to his table. His accent led me to believe he was a Brit, but I soon found out he was actually from New Zealand. He had hitchhiked through England, the homeland of his ancestors, and was on his way back to London to return to Auckland. He was actually flying out of Heathrow the same day as me, so I propositioned him.

"I'm renting a car and driving to London. I'd love to have you join me, be my navigator, and remind me that I need to stay on the wrong side of the road."

He smiled broadly and said, "Actually, it's you Yanks that got things all mixed around—and yes, I'd be delighted to share your car rental to get us to the airport."

"I have a few requirements," I added. "I want to visit a genuine English castle, drive through the Cotswolds and see the Campden cottages, then visit Stratford-upon-Avon on the way."

His charming answer: "My thoughts exactly."

We had a lot in common. Tom was a retired mechanical engineer and loved to "go trekking." He was a meditator and a student of *A Course in Miracles*. The castle was magnificent and the cottages charming; I was particularly fascinated by the canal and canal boats in Stratford. The trip was simply lovely, and the scenery felt strangely familiar. I promised myself

I would return to England one day and travel the canals to spend more time enjoying the English countryside when I was not so engaged trying to navigate roundabouts and shifting gears with my left hand.

This "accidental" encounter led to my next travel adventure. Tom and I traveled so well together and had so much in common that he invited me to come visit him Down Under the next summer. He wanted to show me New Zealand, and it just so happened I had always dreamed of visiting those exotic islands in the Pacific. We exchanged contact information before I dropped him off at the airport and returned the rental car. My flight back home was much faster and less eventful than the trip over. It was a polar flight and flew directly to San Francisco in about twelve hours. I returned to my empty little apartment and began preparing for the next school term.

*To move, to breathe, to fly, to float,*
*To gain all while you give,*
*To roam the roads of land remote,*
*To travel is to live.*

—*Hans Christian Andersen*

*Eleven*

# HARMONIC CONVERGENCE

Shortly after returning home, I got a call from Bruce Alexander, my school administrator, asking me to meet with him and Shirley, my job-share partner, as soon as possible. It seems he was setting up classes for the coming school year and needed to talk to us about our new class assignment. He had already established a day and time with my roommate. I told him I'd be there, hung up, and immediately called Shirley.

"What do you suppose this is all about?" I asked her.

"I don't know, but he probably wants some help placing the Terrible Five with the sixth grade teachers."

"Well, you'd think he could do that over the phone, but it will be good to see you. Let's grab a bite to eat after the meeting and catch up." I hung up, still curious.

Both Shirley and I were mothers of boys and very good at handling the children labeled as the troublemakers of the school. This particular group of boys had been the scourge of Silverwood Elementary since kindergarten and had usually been divided up among the three teachers at each grade level. However, that had changed last school year and we got all five of them. It was a very challenging year. Actually, they were all great kids with loads of energy that needed to be channeled into as much large muscle activity as possible. They were kinesthetic learners and needed to be in the experience of things to be happy in a classroom. Between the two of us,

Shirley and I were able to vary the curriculum sufficiently to keep them very busy and out of Bruce's office.

In the meantime, I checked my to-do list. Number one on the list was to write a letter to Benta, my new young friend in Copenhagen. When I arrived home, there was a letter from her waiting for me. It seems that right after I left her, she made up her mind to leave Denmark and open a crystal shop in Auckland, New Zealand. How synchronistic was that! I could hardly wait to tell her about Tom, my Kiwi traveling companion, and give Benta his contact information. It was such a big world that I was finding it more and more difficult to call these kinds of connections an unusual coincidence.

Next on my list was to contact Lin and Stacey to respond to their special invitation to accompany them along with a few others on a four-day float trip down the Sacramento River. This excursion was to take place during the Harmonic Convergence in the middle of August. Before leaving Denmark, I committed to a year of monthly meetings with the Martins at their home in Novato. It would be a continuation of the work I started in Viborg, but there would be other members for this training I had not yet met.

I was completely clueless as to what a Harmonic Convergence might be and without the internet to help me (remember, this was 1987), I was simply walking through the doors that kept opening to me. Much like the Terrible Five, instead of sitting and trying to get information from books, more and more I was enjoying being in the experience of things. Lin was never still, and he and his "Teacher" were exactly the mentors I needed right now for this leg of my journey, so I accepted this invitation with grateful anticipation.

On the appointed day and time, Bruce met with Shirley and me in one of the small conference rooms next to his office. This drab space did nothing to lessen my trepidation about the encounter. Every time in the past when I had been called in during the summer to discuss my class assignment, it was usually to ask me if I would be willing to take a combination class or teach another grade level. Just two years ago I had agreed to teach a combination third/fourth grade. The children were wonderful, but the double planning and stress of meeting such divergent student needs added to my exhaustion and pain, and eventually led me to request a job-share situation. What did Bruce have in mind for me this year?

"Thank you for coming in, ladies, and I hope you're having a good summer," he greeted us. "I'll get right to the issue at hand. I need you to take your class on to sixth grade. If a parent requests a new placement for their child, I'll honor that request, but with Mary retiring, I need experienced teachers and strong disciplinarians to handle this class, especially now that the Terrible Five are going to be the 'Kings of the Playground.'"

Stunned, I was quiet for a moment. I had never turned down an administrator's request before, but this didn't seem fair. I drew a deep breath and began.

"Bruce, I've taken every assignment asked of me over my twenty-six years of teaching. I've taught second through eighth grade, but the one grade I've never developed curriculum for nor taught is sixth grade. I really do not want to do this," I mumbled with frustration. I could feel the prickle of tears building.

"You only teach half time," Bruce reasoned. "You'll have plenty of time for planning. Besides, you know these kids and they love you."

"I didn't request a job-share situation because I wanted a vacation. I'm doing it because I don't feel good. I simply cannot handle the long hours in the classroom with few breaks and such a large class load. I'm not up to meeting the needs of thirty-five students while developing new programs at this point in my life."

"This is my only viable option. I'm sure the two of you will figure it out."

Always the optimist, Shirley said, "We can do this, Carolyn. I'll help you. Before I started my family, Mary and I used to team-teach sixth grade, so I know the curriculum."

Gathering his folders, Bruce left the room without another word. True to his administrative cloak, he made an executive decision and would not be persuaded otherwise. At lunch that day, Shirley and I agreed that this was Bruce's way of not having to deal with the Terrible Five being constantly sent to his office throughout the next school year.

"Well, I feel used and abused. I've never asked that man for anything, and when I do he makes me feel like I'm shirking my duties as a dedicated public servant. And you have two little ones at home to take care of. I don't want you spending time with me when you could be enjoying your family."

After a really good gripe session about the abuse on the part of our administrator and Shirley's kind reassurances of help, we hugged good-bye and I headed for home feeling a little bit better about the impending assignment. It was now late July, and I would have time in August to get up-to-speed for my new assignment.

August can be blistering hot in California and that year was no exception. I was preparing for my float trip down the Sacramento River to acknowledge and celebrate the Harmonic Convergence. The magazine *Common Ground* had become my faithful published guide to all things metaphysical in my world. The feature article for the August edition was an interview with José Argüelles, who was a professor, author, artist, and visionary scientist. He was instrumental in turning the eyes of the world to the ancient Maya and the importance of what he termed Galactic Time Science. Argüelles's teachings were forming the basis of a harmonic time system inspired by the galactic calendar of the ancient Mayan culture. These intricately engraved stone timepieces were left for us by the ancient Indian tribes of Mesoamerica.

The Harmonic Convergence was to be a lead-up to the global shift Argüelles claimed would happen on December 21, 2012—the ending date for the Mayan Long Count calendar. These engraved stone circles, which tracked the 26,000-year-long cycle of evolution of our planet, was reaching its completion. Argüelles was inviting people to gather, meditate, and perform ceremonies for global peace over a few days during which a rare planetary alignment was to take place. According to Argüelles, this would create a powerful doorway into consciousness. He claimed that any individual who participated would be blessed with an energetic shift. Further, he predicted that participants would receive a foretaste of the energetic changes that would be taking place in the world during the end of 2012. The upshot of all this would be the beginning of a new age of universal peace—a change of the global perspective from one of conflict to one of cooperation. He claimed that this globally synchronized meditation would shift the general vibration of the world. Since my motto was "peace at any cost," I figured participation in this grand experiment was right up my alley. Couldn't hurt, might help.

Lin and Stacey gathered all the kayaks and camping equipment we would need for our four-day sojourn. It took our group about three and a half hours to caravan up I-5 to Shasta Dam, where we embarked on our float down the largest river in California. The Central Valley of the state is fairly flat, so we did not run the risk of having to navigate white water or rapids, but kayaks could tip easily, so we were instructed to bundle our sleeping bags and other necessities in waterproof bags. We actually had to assemble some of the kayaks (Klepper folding kayaks), so while Lin helped us with that task, Stacey had one of the other participants follow her back down the highway, so she could leave one of the vehicles at the place along the river where we would be getting out. Four days floating the river, camping along the way, would take us quite a distance from the dam, and we would need some way to get back to our cars.

With our hats, dark glasses, and sunscreen in position, my young boating partner, Lori, and I pushed off from the bank to begin our adventure. I never met Lori before this trip, but she was a delightful partner. Having grown up on an island, I was experienced with boating and canoeing, but this was my first experience in a kayak and I loved it. You don't sit on a seat in a boat floating on top of the water; you sit or kneel on the bottom of a kayak that is partially submerged in the water. For me the experience was like being one *with* the river. I could feel every ripple and wiggle of the flow as the sleek craft floated the waterway. There was no real exertion paddling other than to simply feather and guide our kayak with the paddles, keeping our craft in the main current.

I don't know how she managed, but Stacey packed enough food to feed us sumptuous vegetarian meals and snacks. We sang songs and told stories around a campfire, then slept out under the stars on isolated islands or sandy promontories for the night. But a lot of that trip was spent in quiet contemplation as we made our way downstream. To myself I began to hum "Row, Row, Row Your Boat" and realized how profound that little childhood ditty actually is. Was this life "all a dream," as the words to the song and *A Course in Miracles* was saying? Was all physical matter a hologram about to collapse with the coming of the new Age of Aquarius? What would appear in its place?

As I navigated it, I began to think of the river as a metaphor for my life at that moment. A river has one purpose—to return its contents back to the sea so it can once again evaporate, become rain, and renew the cycle on our magical water planet. The Sacramento River did this by making its way from the mountains of the High Sierras and Cascades, to the Carquinez Straits near my home in Walnut Creek, flowing into San Francisco Bay, and eventually making its way out into the Pacific Ocean. I began to imagine the ocean representing the vastness of Divine Mind—the All That Is, and the river as my journey through life. If I were more like the river then, when I came up against an obstacle, rather than struggling and pushing against it, I would simply flow around it while keeping my eyes on the purpose of the journey to find my way back to my Source.

Recently, I'd explored changing my name. As tradition dictated, I had taken my husband's surname, Odom, when I married. My students had a heyday with that name: "Oh, isn't she dumb," or "Missus Odor" instead of Mrs. Odom. Aunt Care (née Carolyn Francis Chinn) had mentioned to me that it was a shame her branch of the Chinn family would end with her because there had been no boys born to carry the name forward. I knew she'd be thrilled if I adopted the Chinn name for at least the remainder of my lifetime. However, when I researched my father's surname and my birth name, Bourns, I found the original English spelling had been B-o-u-r-n-e. It seems that because Bourne was such a common name in England, my pioneer ancestor had changed the "e" to an "s" when he immigrated to America in the 1850s. This way his descendants could follow the family line in the New World. The name Bourne originated from England's ancient Anglo-Saxon culture. It originates from a description for a family living at or near a local stream or spring. The connection to water was compelling enough to help me make up my mind and take back my maiden name, Carolyn Ruth Bourns. I would return to my new life with the wisdom of the river to guide me.

On Sunday the 16th of August, I sat in meditation as Lin and his "Teacher" guided us in the proscribed and recommended spans of time that had been publicized. Keeping an open mind, I followed through and performed the same activities, meditating and contemplating on the 17th as well, as we continued down the river. I gladly contributed my time and energy to the Harmonic Convergence. I'm still wondering when the promised Golden Age will arrive, but due to what was soon to follow I know it will.

*May what I do flow from me like the river,*
*no forcing and no holding back...*
*the way it is with children.*
*Then in these swelling and ebbing currents,*
*These deepening tides moving out, returning,*
*I will sing you as no one ever has,*
*streaming through widening channels into opening seas.*

*—Rainer Maria Rilke*

*This is Mom, Barney and me at age 3, taken right before Dad deployed to Europe.*

*Lee, taken in 1984.*

*Michael and Richard, taken in 1988.*

*Idaho cabin with deck in progress.*

*Me with my Aunt Care (Carolyn Francis Chinn), taken in 1989.*

*My father and cousin Brenda in the attic of the big house with his train collection.*

*Stacey and Lin Martin in their Klepper kayak going through the locks at Silkeborg, Denmark.*

*The author in Fiji. "Dr. Livingstone, I presume."*

*Proud Mom and Mike at my 1999 JFK University*
*graduation—a master's degree in Consciousness Studies.*

*Part III*

# LATE WINTER 1988
# TO WINTER 1989

## *Twelve*

# TOUCHING THE HEM

It was a busy fall and winter. With the stress of going back into the classroom, all my symptoms returned and then some. However, my bladder issues were resolved by a very innovative urologist who administered installations of DMSO directly into my bladder. DMSO (dimethyl sulfoxide) is used by veterinarians to alleviate swelling due to trauma, especially in horses. It acts as a carrier to deliver anti-inflammatory medications into the deeper layers of tissue in my bladder. This was an extremely uncomfortable procedure, but I was determined to reverse my symptoms of pain and the constant urgency to void. Interstitial cystitis is the only human condition with Federal Drug Administration (FDA) approval for the use of DMSO in humans. Even topically, when this liquid is applied anywhere on or in the body, an annoying side-effect is the taste and smell of rotten garlic, which takes about twenty-four hours to dispel. I made sure my series of appointments were scheduled late on Friday afternoons, so I would have the weekend alone in my apartment to absorb and then eliminate this horse liniment. I felt extremely blessed that this extraordinary intervention actually worked and my bladder symptoms never returned.

I was not so fortunate in addressing my digestive issues, however. A colonoscopy was ordered by my internist to see if closer examination could help get to the bottom of my GI distress. In the late '80s, the technology was not nearly as sophisticated and refined as it is today. The scope was large and not very flexible, and patients were not given anesthesia to relax them. My cranky colon was not happy with this action plan and spasmed violently at the intrusion. The specialist simply pushed harder. At the conclusion, with tears streaming down my face, I asked him why the procedure was so painful.

"Most people experience mild discomfort, but your bowel just kept spasming," was his brilliant response.

"I would think your logical conclusion would be to withdraw," I shot back. "Obviously, this mechanical procedure was something my bowel objected to in the only way it knew how."

As I dressed to leave, my monkey mind screamed at me. Why did I subject myself once again to such barbaric medical abuse, all to no avail? Why would one crazy horse liniment treatment work and this one wouldn't? Nothing suspicious was found, and I was sent away with instructions to take an over-the-counter remedy called Metamucil. According to this gastroenterologist, my gut was lazy from not consuming enough fiber. Well, I should have known better than to take his advice. The psyllium husk in the Metamucil irritated my inflamed gut lining even more, and my poor beleaguered bowel shut down for days. I was miserable, lost more weight, and regressed back to square one.

This setback lead me to despair. Mealtime, instead of being a period of my day to relax and connect with friends and family, became an activity of dreaded anticipation. So many things I tried to eat seemed to cause further distress, and I was back to consuming only steamed white rice and cooked carrots. I was also concerned about a suspicious lump forming in my right lower abdominal area. I was so thin now that it was not difficult to detect any sort of growth or swelling in my body. This lump was in the area of my right ovary, so I decided to once again consult a gynecologist—this time a woman. After palpating the area she said she wanted to obtain a biopsy, but she was concerned about performing surgery because of my low weight. I thanked her for her input, dressed, and never returned.

Rejecting medical intervention is not necessarily my advice to anyone else, but it seemed obvious to me by this point that I had manifested conditions in my body similar to the way my parents had died: Mom with ovarian cancer; Dad with colon cancer and the complications that followed surgery. Was there more to this mind/body connection than I had ever imagined or dared to believe? My information from the books I was reading said healing was meant "to make whole or holy." What part did I need to gather to me or let go of to become whole? My heart was telling me the responsibility to heal was mine alone and an important part of my journey. I must stop looking for intervention outside myself for true healing to take place. The Buddhist monk Pema Chödrön is quoted as saying: "Nothing ever goes away until it has taught us what we need to know." Obviously, I had not yet learned what my body was trying to teach me.

In spite of the level of pain and exhaustion I was experiencing by the end of my work week, I faithfully attended my monthly weekend trainings with the Martins at their Novato home. These two fascinating individuals always had a well-planned agenda for our group of about ten participants. Stacey served us wonderful meals on Saturday and Sunday which, sadly, I was apprehensive about eating. Since my home was over an hour drive from Novato, I brought my sleeping bag and slept out on their patio or in one of the spare bedrooms Friday and Saturday night and drove back to my apartment in Walnut Creek late Sunday afternoon.

On one particular weekend in early March, when the weather was just beginning to warm, I set out for the Novato training. I didn't mind the long drive because much of it was following the northern shoreline of San Pablo Bay through a national wildlife refuge. I was fascinated by the display of water birds along the way: pure white egrets striking a majestic pose in shallow water, ready to spear an unsuspecting meal; diving ducks bobbing on top of the water, exposing their tail feathers occasionally as they peered below the surface for fish; and groups of sandpipers racing across the mud flats in search of insects and worms. All of this framed by Mount Tamalpais off in the distance.

As I drove, my mind drifted back to my summer adventure on the Sacramento River and the Harmonic Convergence. The promise of organizer José Agüelles had been that those who participated in this two-to-three-day event would be blessed with *an energetic shift in consciousness.* Participation was also described as "giving a foretaste of the energetic changes that would be taking place in the world during the time of the end of the Mayan calendar in 2012." Further, our participation would "open the doors of perception and lift the veils that kept people in separation."

Well, most of our small group attending the Martins' weekend sessions had taken part in the ceremonies and meditations as described, but since that time, none of us had reported anything out of the ordinary. Even though 2012 was a long way off, I was curious about the truth of these claims. Was this whole convergence thing a hoax, or were we in store for great changes in consciousness, possibly in my lifetime?

This was the issue I was grappling with as I pulled up in front of the Martin residence and joined the group inside. Our sessions were held in a large recreation room at the back of the house. That Friday night, we sat in a U formation on the floor, BackJack chairs supporting us. Lin entered into trance allowing that loving collective to speak through him. Teacher's message that evening was particularly memorable, because the topic dealt directly with the issue of separation.

Teacher spoke of a time that would conceivably have existed before what astrophysicists are now calling the 'Big Bang'—their term for the creation of the Cosmos. The logical next question would be: "What came before the Big Bang to cause such a cataclysmic event?" According to Teacher, all that existed before the creation of matter was conscious awareness—the I Am—in the non-body form of spirit. Over eons, the Divine Mind became lonely and decided to create separate souls within the Oneness to expand Creation. The result of this separation was the Big Bang, which eventually evolved into the matter that makes up the galaxies and solar systems of the Cosmos.

According to the creation story Teacher was relating, our separated souls created a veil of forgetfulness, and we could no longer remember ourselves as aspects of the Creator. Our spirits still remembered our divine connection—our Higher or True Self—that looks out upon the material world with spiritual eyes. In that state we see nothing but love, harmony and authenticity. However, humanity now looked out at the material world with only physical eyes, and in that confused state the ego was created. The ego state of our separated souls sees a world of pride, anger, and intolerance.

When we forget or deny our connection to our true self, these negative aspects prevail.

Teacher went on to remind us of the first law of thermodynamics, which states: "Energy cannot be created nor destroyed, but it can be transformed." According to quantum physics, when scientists were able to conduct experiments that took them into the sub-atomic realm of matter, there was nothing there but what seemed to be empty space. It is now estimated that all matter is made up of 99.9999999 percent empty space. The next weird finding of this deeper look into matter was that it takes a conscious observer to transform waves of energy frequency into particles to form substance the human eye can detect.

We must take care of and respect the physical body, but it is merely our earth suit—a bag of cells that has the ability through our five senses to give our souls a human experience. Instead, we have become body identified, and actually think we are a body. We are constantly engaged by an inner critic (the ego) that judges and condemns our actions and keeps us continually drawing from memories of horrible things from the past and projecting the emotions these memories provoke out into the future to create worry, fear, and more separation. The result of this ego strategy is to keep us from experiencing the peace of the present moment. When we are not present, we have no power to change anything in our life. In a state of fear, humans are easily controlled by false gods, whether it be in the form of a priest, a president, or a personified deity. In a state of fear, we cannot distinguish truth from falsehood.

At the conclusion of the session, Teacher made a statement that seemed deeply personal to me: "The assumption of separateness is what leads one to illness." My life, except when I was very young, was based upon the assumption that I am separate and autonomous—an island unto myself. Therefore, I gave little consideration to any issues much greater than my own personal needs and those of my students and loved ones. Now, I was being shown I had potential far beyond my insular false-self. Those thoughts emanating from my ego kept me in judgment of myself and others. No wonder peace of mind was so elusive! How could there be peace when the ego was in charge? Meditation was becoming my practice to make friends with the intellectual part of myself, my pesky ego. Meditation brought me out of the noise of ego and carried me to a state of neutral, so

I could become the observer of my egoic chatter and not constantly under the influence of its caution and criticism. Developing this relaxed state allowed me to re-enter the everyday reality and view it with spiritual eyes that communicated through the heart as wisdom and the gut as intuition. If I allowed my thinking intellect to take over and run the show, I would not heal.

Saturday morning dawned bright and crisp. We ate breakfast and set out for a short hike. The trails on the ridge behind the house meandered through chaparral habitat, oak, and occasional pine trees. My thin body was warmed by a weak sun and delighted in the surround sound of occasional birdsong. I breathed in the scent of leaf fall and soil still moist from winter rain as I huffed and puffed up the steep incline. The glorious view at the top was worth the effort. Our group rested at the top, and I found a magnificent live oak to sit beneath, resting my spine against its rough and weathered bark. When I am asked about my religious orientation, I reply that nature is my cathedral and I must attend it often to be rejuvenated. That was exactly the feeling I had that morning as we descended the trail and returned to the house.

We gathered once again in the recreation room and assumed our U formation, with Lin sitting up front. He told us we would be guided in a chakra meditation. Before we started, Lin warned there might be some noise and distraction due to a recent scheduling of newspaper collection in the neighborhood. He said our challenge would be to use the noise to simply move ourselves deeper into the meditative state. "Each sound," he intoned hypnotically, "will take you deeper and deeper into meditation."

Our group settled, spines straight and eyes closed as Lin began to describe the base chakra. This first energy vortex of the body vibrates to the color red and helps us with issues of survival. Its location is at the base of our spine. Lin slowly described possible life challenges that might affect the function of this primitive energy center before he moved on. The second chakra resonates to the vibration of the color orange and is associated with issues of money, sex, and power in the outside world. The description of second chakra issues were all too familiar to me. I could see why my body had manifested so much personal discomfort in this lower abdominal area of my body.

It was at this point in the late morning's activity that the thumping and banging began to take place outside the house while the collection crew passed through the neighborhood. As suggested, I used this noise to simply move more deeply into a meditative state as I followed the rise and fall of my breath. We were guided gently up to the third chakra, the color of yellow, and the energy center for personal power. Here boundaries are formed and we begin the process of honoring self and feeling compassion for our journey through life. Lin described the purpose of the lower three energy centers as a lifeline to help us safely navigate through the illusory world of matter. Our fourth chakra is the bridge we must cross to carry us up into the higher three spiritual vortices. The fifth, sixth, and seventh chakras connect us back to Spirit. The color of the fourth chakra is green, and it powers the energy center of the heart—the place of unconditional love and wisdom, and the gateway to Spirit.

It was at this point in the morning's meditation that I left the room—not physically, but in conscious awareness. I was gently pulled into the Light as I entered into the Oneness. All was eternal timelessness, possibly best described as spiritual rapture. It was pure ecstasy to escape the straightjacket of my pain-wracked body and the insanity of the separated state—to be gently ushered into the vastness of the Cosmos. How amazing it felt!

Silence,

Freedom,

Connection, so sweet!

And the feeling—verbalizing cannot truly do justice to my experience, but it was happening. How does one put into words a state that is out of this world?

I don't know how long this extraordinary experience lasted, for time does not exist in the place my consciousness had taken me. However, just as suddenly as this experience had drawn me into another Reality, a fissure ripped through the light and vibration that bathed me and a thought seeped into my consciousness.

*I still have work to do. I must return.*

Deep grief swept over me and tears began to stream down my face as my ecstatic state began to dissolve and I returned to my 'normal' state and the room in which I sat. Once again I became aware of Lin's voice just as he was bringing the group out of meditation. The first thing he did was apologize for conducting such a long meditation (about forty-five minutes), but he explained his guides kept insisting he lengthen the activity. Usually, at the end of a guided meditation, Lin checked in with the group for insights and visions people might have received from the activity. Right away his attention was pulled in my direction as he picked up on my state of abject grief.

"Carolyn, are you all right?"

"I had to come back," I mumbled as I grappled to put into words what I had just experienced. "The room dissolved. Everybody was gone and there was nothing but light ... and feeling ... and knowing. I became everything and nothing. I didn't want to come back, but I couldn't stay."

Lin smiled and replied, "That is what's known as 'touching the hem,' and the 'paradox of the divine.' It's a moment of grace that transforms—a true gift to those of us doing the hard work in form. Congratulations."

The group turned to gaze at me. I heard someone comment, "Beginner's luck."

At that point, I struggled to my feet and exited the meeting room to reach the privacy of my bedroom. As I lay on my sleeping bag, every inch of my body vibrated as I closed my physical eyes and assumed a fetal position.

*Why was I cast out once again? All I want is to return Home—back to connection and the ecstatic feeling of being at one with the All That Is.*

I mourned and wept for what seemed like hours, still vibrating from my recent out-of-this-world encounter. Exhausted by ego-driven emotions, I finally surrendered to feelings of gratitude and appreciation for a promise delivered. I participated with all my heart and soul in the recommended rituals of the Harmonic Convergence and the promise was fulfilled. This experience was "a foretaste of the energetic changes that would be taking place in the world during the time of the end of the Mayan calendar in 2012." Even more than a foretaste of things to come was the release from fear of my own mortality. Through this experience, I know my body may dissolve back into the oneness, but my conscious knowing is infinite.

My heart was telling me I still had curriculum to complete in Earth School before I could graduate and return Home. The 'end time,' or promised Golden Age, was still at least twenty-five years in the future. My recent experience was simply a taste of what that future might be if I stayed and healed my body, while serving as a bridge to help others discover their connection to Spirit.

*You believed you could transcend the body as you aged,*
*she tells herself.*
*You believed you could rise above it, to a serene,*
*nonphysical realm.*
*But it's only through ecstasy you can do that,*
*and ecstasy is achieved through the body itself.*
*Without the bone and sinew of wings, no flight.*
*Without that ecstasy you can only be dragged further down*
*by the body, into its machinery.*
*Its rusting, creaking, vengeful, brute machinery.*

—*Margaret Atwood,*
Stone Mattress: Nine Wicked Tales

*Thirteen*

# DOWN UNDER

The end of the school year was fast approaching. As extraordinary as my early spring experience was, not much changed in my day-to-day struggle with pain and fatigue. There is a Zen proverb that sums it up very nicely: "Before Enlightenment, chop wood, carry water. After Enlightenment, chop wood, carry water." My rational mind could make no sense of the experience, let alone find the words to describe it. At just the moment paradise was obtained, I had to go through the agony of realizing it was lost. What did this mean?

My enlightenment experience was a devastating attack on my ego and a huge challenge to what I previously considered a 'rational' view of life. As my old beliefs crumbled, it felt like I was floundering in a sea of paradox. I had spent my life up to this point building up inventories of information and "facts," only to discover that in the end I must throw it all away. Pain and suffering will cease only when I realize that it will never cease. The next step on my journey was accepting the final realization that nothing is really known, and nothing really needs to be known. My journey is both the dark night of the soul and the way to freedom and paradise. I must accept paradox for the mystery it is and simply move forward with my life.

Summer was on its way along with the promise of new adventures. I corresponded with the friends I made while in Europe the summer before. Benta, my Danish friend, had moved to Auckland, opened her business, and was now fast friends with Tom, the gentleman I would soon be touring with in New Zealand. My previous trip abroad had been pretty well planned out for me by others in my group, but this time I was striking out on my own. I contacted an acquaintance of mine who was a fellow "empty nester." Like me, Karen had gotten married while earning her college degree, but she stayed at home with her children while they were growing up. Now that all three kids had flown the nest, she retrained as a travel agent and was starting to take on clients.

Karen was very excited for me when I shared my plans for travel to the South Pacific. By coincidence, Qantas Airways had recently announced a special offer to people traveling from the western United States to and from Australia in celebration of Brisbane hosting the World's Fair in '88. There was an eight hundred dollar ticket that would fly me to seven different locations where Qantas maintained service, so long as it was one continuous loop ending in the city of my departure. My original plan was to visit only Australia and New Zealand, but this airline special offered a whole new set of exotic possibilities. Since it would be late fall and winter Down Under, I decided that stopping off in some tropical locations might be "just the ticket." Another exciting possibility was to visit one of the South Pacific islands that still supported an indigenous population, so I could visit a local elementary school and set up a pen pal exchange for my classroom next school term.

After studying my options, Karen arranged for departure from San Francisco, changing planes in Hawaii, and on to my first destination—the city of Nadi on the Fijian Island of Viti Levu. I would have six days in this tropical island paradise before I continued my journey on to Sidney, Australia. I was clear I wanted to avoid Brisbane and the crowds expected there, but I was very interested in the more tropical part of Australia to the north. Cairns, the Great Barrier Reef, and the Atherton Tablelands seemed like the perfect choice. After another week exploring this area, I would be back on the plane to keep my rendezvous with Tom and Benta in New Zealand. Tom planned a three-week itinerary through both the north and south islands for us that would include lots of "trekking." My last stop would be back to Honolulu to enjoy four days on Oahu before returning to San Francisco.

The previous year I discovered that too much advanced planning often limits spontaneous opportunities, so I simply gathered information on the location of youth hostels and visitor's centers in the cities into which I was flying. For my accommodations, I decided to take pot luck along the way. My next challenge was to pack winter clothes for Australia and New Zealand and summer clothes for Fiji, Cairns, and Oahu.

I do not sleep well on jets, so it was nice to have interesting fellow passengers to talk to on my overnight flights. Such was the case on the Hawaii to Fiji leg of my journey. My seatmates were both young Australian boys, and we carried on a lively conversation until we all three tired and eventually fell asleep.

"We are beginning our descent into Nadi International Airport, and we have been cleared for landing. While you slept we crossed the International Dateline. The date is July 18th and presently the time is 5:06 a.m.," came the cockpit announcement over the intercom.

As we began our descent and continued to receive landing instructions, I turned to my fellow seatmates to give my farewells.

"You're getting off in Nadi?" one of my new young friends asked, as a concerned look spread across his face.

"Yes, I have this amazing ticket that allows me up to seven stops throughout the South Pacific," I responded blithely. "Nadi is my first stop. I'm hoping to set up a letter-writing exchange with a classroom."

"Down Under here, we refer to Nadi as The Armpit of the Pacific. I hope you have somewhere else to go in Fiji."

"Thanks for the heads-up," I responded as I stood to get my things from the overhead compartment. A gentleman sitting in the seat behind me stood to help.

"I thought I heard you say you're getting off here. Did you know Fiji's been under a military coup situation since last year? Recently, a shipment of weapons was intercepted and confiscated off the coast of one of the outer islands by the Fijian military, and things are a bit tense on the islands right now. It appears you're traveling alone. You need to be careful."

"Really? I had no idea! I don't think my travel agent was aware of this interesting travel detail either. I simply want to make friends, not war. I'm sure I'll be fine."

I exited the plane, feeling somewhat apprehensive, then sailed through customs with no problems whatsoever. I retrieved my luggage and entered the main terminal in short order. Everything appeared peaceful, if not unusually quiet for an international airport. I proceeded to the bank kiosk and exchanged $120 American into Fijian currency, then looked around for lockers, so I could stash my winter suitcase. I spotted a Traveler's Information Bureau and headed in that direction. One of the local taxi drivers approached me, hat in hand.

"I am Hussain. How can I help you, lady? What do you need?" I looked carefully at the short, heavyset man in front of me as he smiled broadly.

"Well, I'll be needing someone to take me into Nadi to find accommodations, but right now I'm looking for a locker to store this bag."

I indicated the suitcase that held my hiking boots and winter wardrobe for the month I would be touring Australia and New Zealand. Hussain brightened.

"Beautiful lady, look no further. I, Hussain, will take you into town to the Nadi Hotel. It has fine rooms, good food, and a storeroom for your bag. You will like it very much."

All my immediate needs resolved with one chance encounter seemed too good to be true. I followed Hussain as he commandeered my luggage. Stepping outside the air-conditioned terminal, I was stunned by the heat and humidity of my surroundings. I folded myself into the back of Hussain's little Japanese import, and we headed into Nadi. Armpit, indeed. This drab little settlement was certainly not the paradise I had imagined.

"Hussain, is there any kind of travel bureau in town? I'm interested in learning more about the islands and people of Fiji. I'm a school teacher and would like to arrange to visit a classroom in your country."

"What luck you are in, lady. My cousin, Hakima, arranges trips for visitors all over the islands of Fiji. She will find you a classroom in a village to visit and a nice place to stay. You will see. We will stop by her place on the way to the hotel. No problem."

Cousin Hakima wrote out my travel itinerary in pencil on a scrap of notepaper after making arrangements with an "uncle" on the north island of Vanua Levu. At 4:30 the next morning, I would catch the bus to Ellington Wharf. From there, I would take a ferry to Nabouwalu on the large island to the north, then catch another bus to Saivou, then another bus to Savusavu, where I would stay overnight. The next morning, I would board a bus at 9:00 to Bagasau, where I would be directed to Thomas Baker—the local school teacher in the village of Nakobo. After my two-day stay with the Baker family ($10 per day, all meals included), I would return by way of Savusavu, where I would catch a plane back to the capital city of Suva on the main island, then return by bus across the main island of Viti Levu back to Nadi. To complete my Fiji tour, I would take a day cruise to Beachcomber Island for a *lovo* (Fiji-style luau) and day of fun in the sun. I was set. Let the adventure begin.

*I've not ceased being fearful,*
*I've gone ahead despite the pounding in my heart*
*that says turn back, turn back,*
*You'll die if you go too far.*

—*Erica Jong*

*Fourteen*

# ADVENTURE IN PARADISE

My accommodations at the Nadi Hotel were Spartan but adequate. After about seven hours of fairly good sleep, my travel alarm awakened me at three-thirty the next morning. I had bought fruit and goat cheese at a local outdoor market the day before, which went into my backpack along with water and my trusty Swiss Army knife, my camera, and the clothes I would need for the next few days. I took my other bags to the storage room off the lobby. There was a carved statue standing guard outside the closet-like storeroom. I was told it was capable of protecting my possessions from theft. I sent out a quick feeling of appreciation to this small ferocious-looking idol. It had taken on a mighty task since there was no lock on the door and the room was accessible to all from the lobby. I left my hotel in the dark, using my key-chain flashlight, and made my way on foot to catch the 4:30 bus.

When I arrived at the designated corner, there were a few men sitting on the ground around a bowl containing the local drink—kava kava. Fortunately, I had done some research on the customs of Fiji, so I was somewhat familiar with this unique island beverage. The root of the kava kava plant was chewed, spit into a pot, and then left for a while to ferment. It had numbing and intoxicating effects. The novelty of a solitary female foreigner appealed to the group. They immediately started calling out for me to come join them for a drink. I declined as gracefully as possible and moved closer to a Welsh couple and another young Fijian while we waited for the bus to arrive.

In about ten minutes, the bus came and we loaded on. I sat about halfway back next to a window, so I could see the countryside and coastline as we traveled. Soon the bus began to fill, not just with people of all sorts and descriptions, but with livestock as well—a couple of goats and lots of poultry. Then a *kaivalagi* (Fijian for foreigner) about my age boarded with a rucksack, tripod, and small suitcase. In retrospect, except for the fact there was no bullwhip slung over his shoulder and he was a blond, this man resembled Indiana Jones from the movie *Raiders of the Lost Ark*. He sat down next to the driver, then turned to look at the passengers and spotted me. The next thing I knew, he was leaning over the seat in front of me.

"My God, woman! Where did you come from and what are you doing here?"

"I'm from California, and I'm on my way to Venua Levu to visit a village school for a couple of days. I teach school and I'll be setting up a letter-writing exchange with a Fijian classroom. What brings you out so early this morning?"

"I'm here in Fiji to take video pictures of a large property for some clients of mine in Seattle. It's a 10,000 acre property which is very remote and uninhabited. They planted Caribbean pine on some of the property about twenty years ago. I'm going to photograph the trees and beaches to prepare a publicity presentation in order to sell the property for my client," he explained. "Do you mind if I sit next to you? It's about a two-and-a-half hour trip to the ferry. We can talk."

His name was Gene Hamilton, and he was from San Diego. He turned out to be a frequent visitor to Fiji, so he knew a lot about the islands. He was an actor, writer, artist, inventor, and real estate broker, to name only a few of his many talents.

When I described my itinerary, Gene was aghast. "Good God, woman! You'll be dead by the time you get to Bagasau. Do you know how far that is?"

"Oh, I'm staying overnight in Savusavu, so I'll be just fine. Then I'll be flying from Savusavu to Suva on my return, take a bus back to Nadi, and catch my flight to Sidney on Saturday."

"Well, I'm going to do my best to change your mind."

As Gene settled in next to me, he launched a campaign to get me to go with him on his picture-taking expedition. He even offered me fifty dollars to act as his model for some of the shots he would be taking of the beaches. I declined. He went on to describe how he would be staying in the village of Bua, which was about twenty miles north of Nabouwalu Jetty (the ferry landing). His intention was to find and hire a fishing boat, stay overnight Tuesday, get the pictures Wednesday and stay one more night in Bua, then return to Nadi on Thursday. It would take him a couple of days to get the pictures developed and prepare the presentation once he got back to the States, then he would be flying to Tokyo to offer the property. (Back in the '80s, Japan was enjoying huge economic prosperity, and the Japanese were gobbling up land wherever they could).

When we arrived at Ellington Wharf and loaded onto the ferry, there were a number of Fiji military personnel who were wearing camouflage uniforms and carrying rifles with bandoliers slung over their shoulders. They checked my passport, went through my backpack, and asked my destination. I was allowed to pass after I extracted my handwritten itinerary from my backpack and showed it to them, explaining my intention to find pen pals for my classroom. It took Gene considerably longer to make it through the check point. On the four-hour crossing, I asked him what he knew about the political situation here on these gorgeous tropical islands. Even outside on the deck of the ferry where we were sitting there were uniformed and armed soldiers present.

Gene explained that Fiji had been taken over by Britain about a hundred years earlier. When Britain colonized Fiji, many of the citizens of India and other South Asian British colonial countries followed to become servants to their English "masters." When Fiji gained status as an independent member of the commonwealth in 1970, a bicameral Parliament was established. By this time, two distinct factions existed in this remote island nation: the ethnic Fijian community and the Indo-Fijian contingency. The indigenous population laid claim to about 90 percent of the land and agriculture, while the Indian faction became the business and financial leaders. As the Indo-Fijian population grew in numbers to almost 50 percent of the island's population, the native chiefs realized that they were in jeopardy of being voted out of control of their land, and so they revolted. The current coup by the Fijian military was the result.

This explained why all my contacts, since I had entered the country, were with Indians. All my interactions with locals so far had involved an exchange of money for goods or services. My only contacts with the native Fijians were men dressed in uniforms toting weapons and ammunition. Remembering what I was told before landing—that a whole shipload of weapons was recently confiscated off the coast—it seemed to me a reasonable incentive for the Fiji chiefs to be up in arms. No wonder the military was everywhere.

"What does this mean for your mission?" I asked Gene. "If this 10,000 acres of prime land is still held by foreign interests, I would think the fact that you're looking to sell it off to the Japanese would be of great interest to the Fijian military."

"Well, that's one of the reasons I'm doing this the hard way. I could have just been helicoptered into the property, but there's a Fijian village very close to the bay where the trees were planted. I'm trying to be as inconspicuous as possible, so I don't get picked up by the military. I will appear to be a foreign tourist out fishing for the day. Hopefully, I'll be a tourist with his wife, out fishing for the day." He patted my hand companionably and I returned my best schoolteacher look of disapproval.

He withdrew his hand and continued. "I'm definitely roughing it to carry out this project, but I've got a seaside room reserved and waiting for me at the Regent of Fiji, which is the only really posh hotel near Nadi or anywhere else on the islands for that matter. I'm staying there for two days before I catch my flight back to the States late Saturday."

Then Gene started his "pitch" in earnest. He wanted me to come with him on his picture-taking venture. Then I could accompany him back to his sumptuous accommodations to luxuriate in the spa atmosphere of the Regent of Fiji five-star hotel. Humm. He pointed out we were both flying out on Saturday, so we could even go to the airport together. I was mildly amused by his invitation, but definitely not interested. After all, I had this amazing itinerary all planned and paid for. Why would I choose to change plans?

By now our stomachs were grumbling. We had been up for hours without eating. I whipped out my goat cheese, papaya, and pilot crackers, along with my Swiss Army knife, napkins, and wipes and proceeded to fix us a light breakfast. Definitely not the outdoorsman, Gene had brought canned goods to see himself through the adventure. The big problem was he had forgotten a can opener. I had enough to share, so we snacked on my meager offering with his promise he would buy me a proper meal when we landed in Nobouwalu.

What can I say? By the time we completed our four-hour ferry boat ride to the north island, Gene had charmed me into accompanying him on his adventure. All my objections were to be handled once we got to our destination. There was a phone and post office in Nobouwalu, where he took care of all the cancelations. Gene promised he would arrange for me to visit a classroom in Bua Village to set up my letter-writing exchange.

The restaurant in Nabouwalu was on the pier where the ferry was unloading vehicles and passengers. As we made our way up the landing, there was a pleasant-looking Indo-Fijian standing by a late model white Toyota truck. Gene went over to him and asked about a ride into Bua Village after we had eaten. The man, who identified himself as Robin, enthusiastically agreed to transport us anywhere we wanted to go. We introduced ourselves, but thereafter Gene became "Boss" and I became "Lady."

It was only about 10:30, so the restaurant had not yet begun to prepare lunch. In the tropics, food spoils quickly, so everything is prepared fresh, including the chicken that had to be caught, killed, and cleaned for our meal. The waiter/cook explained it would take a while, but please be seated. As we watched the ferry unloading, soldiers were once again checking the cars and passengers. Gene was hoping our detour into the restaurant would avoid the hassle of going through the interrogation process one more time.

"Carolyn, I think it would be a good idea if we presented ourselves as husband and wife. We don't want to flaunt these peoples' customs," he added quietly.

I looked at him skeptically, as the door flew open and a huge Fijian soldier loomed over us. He demanded to see our passports and asked questions for about twenty minutes. The careful examination of our passports was the first evidence of how hard the husband-wife ruse was going to be with passports revealing separate last names *and* separate addresses. This evidence certainly did not speak of marital bliss. After our passports were returned and the soldier strode out the door, Gene became rather agitated about the interview.

"It looks like my project is going to be trickier than I figured. A good friend of mine was the most powerful Indian political leader here. He's now living outside the country for his own safety. An interim government was formed after the coup last year. It has revoked the Indians' civil rights. These soldiers are conducting house searches, confiscating personal possessions, including all weapons, and monitoring correspondence on and off the islands. When the Fijian military trumps up a charge against you, they lock you up and throw away the key. The situation is very volatile, especially here on the north island where tourists are rarely seen. I can really feel the tension the further we get from Nadi and Suva."

Our food came and we devoured a marvelously tasty meal of chicken, rice, and fresh vegetables that the handwritten menu called chicken chow mein. We were collected by our faithful driver, Robin, a loving and energetic man of forty-seven. He carried on an incessant line of chatter and seemed constantly in motion. Robin assured us he could take care of all our needs: we could stay at his home; he knew a captain with a fishing boat; his sister was married to the village "master," and they both taught at the elementary school. His truck, Robin informed us proudly, was the newest and finest on the island. Currently, his wife was away due to a death in her family, and he had two sons at home—little four-year-old Dotti and Vern, who was twenty-two.

Gene and I squeezed into the front seat of Robin's truck, and we drove off the pier along a dirt road to run our errands and make arrangements for our boating adventure the next day. Before we left Nambouwow, Robin took us to *the* public telephone and post office. The structure sat perched atop a hill. You lined up and waited your turn for the phone, then paid your money and a switchboard operator placed the call. While Gene spoke with the airline, I went around to the other side of the structure to mail some postcards. The major task of the day for the postmaster was finding the cost of putting a stamp on my postcard to Henrik in Sweden. I doubt that too many missives had ever been posted to Stockholm from Nambouwow.

As we drove on toward Bua Village, Robin stopped and spoke to or picked up family, friends, and livestock along the way. The back of the truck began to fill with curious villagers. It seemed that few Americans were ever seen in this part of the world. "Fiji time" is an expression used on the islands and it is extremely appropriate. Our driver had a different relationship to time and was not about to be hurried. One hour might be three, months can be years, etc. Our ride through the countryside was fascinating. Villagers on horseback; goats, chickens, and Brahma cows; exotic plants of every variety, height, and color. The houses were modest, with neatly kept yards and lovely gardens. Most of the structures were hand-built and simple in construction. Many were elevated so the livestock could be housed underneath. The structures showed a lot of wear-and-tear from the beating sun, the constant humidity, and the occasional hurricanes of the tropics.

As our driver meandered through the village, he stopped frequently to show us off to relatives and friends. Gene kept trying to get Robin back on track, which was to hire a proper boat for the open sea and set up for the picture-taking expedition the next day. Everywhere we stopped, we had to sit and consume some sort of beverage—sweet tea, coconut milk, or orange juice.

Eventually we arrived at the Captain's house. It was a typical Fijian *bure*, which is the traditional wood- and mat-sided, thatched-roof structure with dirt floor. The Captain was an interesting man. His looks might be described as country bumpkin, with a somewhat slouched stature and noticeable overbite. Below the outward appearance was a highly shrewd, charming, and intelligent gentleman. He had a large piece of choice land and owned a tractor, fishing boat, truck, etc. and was considered very prosperous by his neighbors.

We found out later that the delay in arriving at the Captain's house was because he had been held by the Fiji military, where he was detained and interrogated for two days, even though he surrendered his rifle as ordered by the interim government. Gene made a deal with the Captain to take us to the property for $150 and gas. The man was ecstatic. On this island, daily wages were about two dollars. His boat had a small cabin and a thirty horse-powered outboard motor. We were taking it out into the open ocean, and there were no life preservers anywhere in sight. Gene assured me these people were expert boatmen and we would be safe since we would be following the coast.

Our last stop was to meet Robin's school-teacher sister. Her husband also taught and acted as the master (principal) of Bua Village School. They had a ten-year-old daughter, Satya, who would be accompanying us back to Robin's house to act as stand-in for Robin's missing wife. I immediately fell in love with this precious child. She had the enthusiasm and innocence of her uncle, but offered it with intelligence and reserve. It became her job to cook for the whole crew and watch after her little nephew, Dotti. I was not allowed to lift a finger, although I would have been much more comfortable if I could have helped.

On our way at last to the house, Robin stopped one more time to pick up his nephew, Bridgemont. This dear young man, probably in his mid-thirties, helped his uncle entertain us and accompanied us on our boating adventure. Powerfully built, Bridgemont possessed a good sense of humor and cheerful disposition. He was very kind and thoughtful toward me during my stay in these unique and sometimes challenging surroundings.

We did not get back to the house until almost dark. The sun sets about 6:30 in the tropics. A live chicken was brought from Bridgemont's house for our dinner, and Gene bought some prawns from the local store when we stopped for gas in Bua Village. Vern and Satya prepared our dinner while the rest of us sat out on the patio behind the house, visiting and drinking warm Fiji beer that Bridgemont had recently managed to procure on the black market.

Our enterprising host owned a fine home by Fijian standards. Upon our arrival we were shown our sleeping quarters—a tiny room off the living room. Robin had commandeered Vern's bed, which was a twin-sized pallet on the floor with mosquito netting over it. We were told to put our belongings there. They assumed we were a couple, and I was getting extremely apprehensive about what I had gotten myself into.

The inside of the house was divided into small rooms, but most activity was conducted in the outdoor area between the cooking shed and the main house. Cooking was done in a structure separate from the main house over an open fire surrounded by cinder brick. A pine log was lit at one end and fed into the fire as needed. It was very smoky and only one item was cooked at a time. Robin was very proud of the fact that he had a single electrical line coming into the house to operate a refrigerator. We were informed it was one of the few modern appliances on the island. It was quite a distance away from the outdoor kitchen, but that was the cook's problem.

Water was supplied by a central outdoor spigot where you collected what you needed in buckets for personal use. The shower (cold water only) was outside at the back of the house, where I encountered one of the largest spiders it has ever been my dubious honor to meet. I was informed that this humongous creature was encouraged to take up residence in the corner of the shower to keep the insects from attacking our naked bodies. The size of this arachnid was testimony to the abundance of insects in the immediate area.

The climate and volcanic soil was so lush in this tropical environment that it only takes a few years for a banana or coconut palm to mature and bear fruit and only a few weeks for vegetables to grow. All nutritional needs were supplied by plants that surrounded the house, with the exception of staples like rice, wheat, spices, etc. Papaya, or pawpaw as they are called on the islands, grow as large as watermelons and are delicious. I picked one I could reach to take on our boating expedition the next day. I noticed that a large divot, reaching deep into the flesh, had recently been made in the fruit. I was informed that a fruit rat had taken a bite. This helped the locals to know the pawpaw was ripe and ready to eat. Coconuts were everywhere and used for every imaginable purpose, but mainly as feed for livestock.

The bathroom was of the "drop and squat" variety, and toilet paper was an unknown nicety. A can of water next to the hole in the ground served this purpose. There were also a number of colorful and very large tropical toads that inhabited the enclosure. Again, the toads are encouraged to keep down the insect population, but their bodies are highly toxic, so I was told not to touch them. (Fat chance!) The position one had to assume to hit the hole and the stare of huge toady eyes made eliminations extremely challenging. I preferred using the bushes, but never knew what I might encounter in the jungle just beyond the clearing for the yard.

While dinner was being prepared, we sat around and talked. I was politely included in all discussions with the men, not as an equal but as a woman. Gene was a tough act to follow and loved an audience. As the conversation grew thin, he disappeared into his room and came out with a red handkerchief. He made it disappear in his hand and then reappear again. This simple act of magic enthralled his audience—Vern, Bridgemont, Robin, Satya, and little Dotti. It was wonderful watching the faces of both the children *and* adults as Gene spun his web of illusion. I was fascinated by their reaction. They were absolutely rapt—laughing, amazed and thoroughly enjoying themselves—and then the military crashed our little party.

Two very large Fijians dressed in military uniforms carrying weapons and ammunition entered the lantern-lit outdoor area where we were gathered. Gene stepped forward to greet them and shook hands.

The spokesman's opening comment was, "I think you know why I'm here."

Gene hesitated for but a moment. "No, I really don't" was his level response.

What proceeded was an hour-long interrogation, with our passports carefully scrutinized, followed by thorough questioning about our purpose for being there in that house at that time. Gene was as truthful as possible with only a few omissions, like the fact that his purpose was to sell off 10,000 acres of prime Fijian real estate to foreigners. Our husband and wife ruse was exposed with the examination of our passports, so I was able to be the wide-eyed and innocent elementary school teacher eager to orchestrate a cultural exchange for my classroom back home.

Gene carried on marvelously as he waxed nostalgic about all his time in the islands. His performance was even better than the magic act the interrogation had interrupted. The interrogator was very slow and deliberate. He probably smelled a rat as Gene rambled on. Strangely, I was not particularly worried, but could sense that Gene was nervous. I began to concentrate on sending peace, love, and light to the drama being played out before me. I spoke only when directly asked a question. There was great relief all around when the two soldiers finally stood to leave.

Our dinner had been on hold for over an hour and was finally served and eaten as we all tried processing what had just taken place. Bridgemont was starting to feel his beer and was the only one beside Gene and me to show emotion or concern. After we ate, the men went outside to take care of some matter of concern that I was not privileged to know about at that time. It was very late when we finished eating and we had a 6:30 wake-up for our picture-taking mission the next day. Fortunately, Satya had picked up on the fact that sleeping arrangements were awkward and went about setting up a pallet and netting for me on the floor in the living room—one difficult problem solved by a very astute young girl!

Sleep did not come easily after such a long and tense day, and every little noise awakened me. The whole household woke up at 4:00 for Dotti to take a trip to the potty. I never did get back to sleep. About six in the morning, Gene lifted my netting and lay down beside me. He gave me a nice back rub down the spine with the promise of more to come.

We had breakfast of fish and rice, then packed for the adventure before us—lunch things, video equipment and cameras, fishing gear, sunscreen, etc. It was eight o'clock before we finally got out on the water. The day was calm but overcast, and Gene was afraid he would not get very good pictures. I assured him the sun would be shining by the time we made our way up the coast to the property. We proceeded without incident, noting beautiful untouched beaches along the way. Shots were difficult to take because of the sun's position, which broke through the overcast not too long after we left the launch site.

It took us more than an hour to get to the edge of the estate. Gene was anxious to get to the deep water harbor at the end of the property. Altogether we were on the water for almost four hours before we arrived at the bay where the trees had been planted. We stopped a couple of times, but we had the wind at our backs. I anticipated an arduous return trip as we would be going against the prevailing wind. The harbor and the hill with the pines rather reminded me of Mount Konocti, a volcanically formed peak at the end of Clear Lake in California. There was a Fijian village on the left side of the bay and a lovely beach further down to the far left of the village. Captain said that beach belonged to his brother, and we could stop there on our way out and have lunch. We took plenty of pictures, then headed past the Fijian village to the beach to enjoy our meal together on dry land.

We had just gotten underway when a fast-moving outboard departed from the dock at the Fijian village and headed in our direction. The passenger in the front of the boat waved vigorously and we all waved back. We got over to the beach before the outboard finally overtook us. The occupants were one very large, very irate Fijian chief, along with his driver. The hand wave we had previously been given was to stop us, *not* a friendly hello. Again we went through the questions, and Gene proceeded with his song and dance. When they finally departed, we ate quickly and were once again on our way. Gene was really upset by the constant harassment and the changes that had taken place in this island paradise.

As I anticipated, the return trip was not nearly as smooth. As the wind kept pounding us back, the four of us inched forward through very rough seas. Gene and I were on the deck of the boat to act as ballast for a smoother ride. Soon both of us were beginning to blister from the intense tropical sun and glare off the water. For some reason, I had been guided to bring a length of fabric I'd purchased at the market in Nadi before I left on this trip. We draped it over our lily-white bodies and had quite a conversation. It was in this safe and intimate enclosure that Gene shared with me what had taken place last night after dinner. The other men helped him bury a bayonet he had foolishly hidden in his luggage to bring on this adventure. He shared that he was sweating bullets, fearing that the soldiers who came to the house the night before would search his belongings and find it. Gene was convinced that, had I not been with him, he would now be cooling his heels in a Fijian prison.

As we continued around the peninsula, the wind really kicked up and soon there were waves breaking over the bow of the boat. We had to sit toward the stern, getting totally drenched. For over an hour and a half we traveled in this manner, with me huddled up against Gene, singing rainy day songs, reciting poetry, telling dirty jokes—anything to keep our spirits up and mind off our discomfort. The sea water was not cold, but the constant drenching and wind soon chilled me thoroughly.

About the time I thought we should be reaching the landing, Captain stopped the boat one more time to catch fish. Gene and I only wanted to get to dry land, not forage for dinner. Bridgemont told us the tide was not high enough yet to access the inlet where the dock was located. I was devastated. All I wanted was to get off the water, put on dry clothes, and warm up. Not only that, but we were informed it would be another forty minutes to our dock site. The men did catch about a three pound rock cod, and we were intercepted one more time by a boat load of Fijians. These men did not speak English, so the crew had to act as interpreters. I was sitting uncomfortably inside the cabin by now, trying to keep out of the wind, and decided not to even bother explaining why I was there.

When we finally got to the inlet, the tide was still too far out, so Captain waded into shore and walked home to call Robin. We waited another forty minutes or more as the sun began to set. I had camped outdoors enough to know dusk meant mosquitoes! It began sounding like a Boeing 747 preparing for take-off in the mangrove surrounding the inlet. I informed the men sitting in the boat that I was not going to be eaten alive waiting for the tide to come in, so I whipped out my little flashlight, waded to the bank and slipped along the muddy trail back to the dock. Gene was close behind. Our timing was perfect. Robin pulled up with the truck just as we reached the dock. We piled into the truck and slammed the door just as the mosquitoes swarmed out of the swampy area we had navigated moments before.

My carry-all and money belt were now drenched with salt water and covered with mud and pawpaw. Sea salt was crystalized and caked on my neck, face, and arms and in my hair. I shuddered, remembering I had only a cold water shower and a very large spider awaiting me back at the house to remedy my current discomfort.

After we showered, both of us lay down on Gene's bed to rest. Gene fell off into a deep sleep almost immediately. I could hear people arriving, so I got up to be with them. I figured Gene was done for the night. I could see that dinner was going to be another major happening, especially since Satya's parents had joined us. I did my best at small talk with everyone, but was fading fast. About that time, Gene popped his head out the door, rested, refreshed, and ready to charm. He was carrying his video camera on one shoulder. The entertainment for the evening was Gene videotaping the family as they panned for the camera, and then showing them their images and antics on the little playback window on the back of the camera. A good time was had by all and dinner was finally served, again at 10:30.

After dinner, Gene did card tricks, and Satya and I exchanged addresses for setting up pen pals with her class and my new class of sixth graders waiting to meet me upon my return to the States. Gene spoke with Satya's father about messages and codes to communicate outside the country just in case things got really bad in paradise. My fervent wish was for peace and continued happiness for this loving and generous family.

By way of epilogue to my Fiji adventure, on our way back to Nadi, Gene decided he wanted to preview the videos he had taken of the property the day before. To his horror, he discovered the videos of the property had inadvertently been recorded over when he'd videotaped the family and their antics the night before. The only saving grace was that I had taken my trusty Canon Sureshot with me on the boat. I'd taken lots of still shots as we followed the beaches along the property. Once the film was developed, Gene thought he could probably use these still photos for his presentation. I turned two rolls of film over to him at the airport, and he promised to send me the duplicates when he arrived back home. He saw me off at the gate, and I continued on to Australia. When I got home there was a package waiting for me. He had taken the film to a one-hour developing location that had eaten up one of the rolls. The remaining roll of developed photos in the envelope contained mostly pictures of the family and Bua Village. I never heard from Gene again.

*No one is born hating another person*
*because of the colour of his skin,*
*or his background or his religion.*

*People learn to hate,*
*and if they can learn to hate,*
*they can be taught to love,*
*for love comes more naturally*
*to the human heart than its opposite.*

*—Nelson Mandela*

*Fifteen*

# A-HA MOMENT

As memorable as my adventure on Fiji turned out to be, it was my impression of exotic beauty and the infinite variety Down Under I still hold close to my heart—the exotic panorama of the land masses of the South Pacific. Relishing the gardens; a stroll along deserted tropical beaches; the power and eternal motion of wind and wave of the Coral Sea—bobbing weightlessly above the surface as I dip my mask underwater to reveal the kaleidoscope of sea creatures inhabiting the Great Barrier Reef; the power of a raging river throwing me about as I wend my way down its cascading length; the rainforest of the Atherton Table Lands stretching above black basalt columns reaching high above my head; a flash of brilliant blue butterfly wings, hidden birds and bandicoots calling out to their kind.

But I was back now to the stark reality of my dismantled life. I could flee to a tropical paradise for a brief respite from the grind of survival, but I could not escape myself and my cranky body. Because I was job-sharing, I was off for a solid week, then in the classroom teaching every day for the next week. Even though I was not working full time, I spent a lot of time coordinating curriculum with my job-share partner, Shirley. I would just begin to feel better on my week off to then fall back into the same symptoms by the end of my week in the classroom. I simply could not seem to keep up with what used to be a challenging, creative, and fulfilling profession. What was I missing? Peace of mind was all well and good, but how could I feel inner peace when my body was in such distress? No matter what I did to soothe my mind, improve my diet and lifestyle, I continued to be plagued with fatigue and pain. Obviously, I was still missing something important to bring about my healing, but I was mystified as to what that might be.

I made it through September and October, but things began to really fall apart in November. As the days grew shorter and the weather chilled, my symptoms began to worsen. By the end of November, my bowels shut down and nothing I tried seemed to help get things moving again. I didn't dare keep putting food in my body when nothing would come out, so I stopped eating and simply drank warm liquids. On day eight of my body's rebellion, my monkey mind began to chatter as I grew weaker and more frantic.

*This is not normal. I feel so achy and toxic. What if my bowel perforates like it did with Dad? The doctors have nothing to offer and I simply don't know where to turn any more for relief. What did I do to deserve such misery?*

With pain tearing at my gut and every joint in my body aching, I stumbled into my bedroom, sank down on my knees at the foot of my bed and cried out for forgiveness to a God who was surely punishing me for leaving my sick husband. I sobbed to the point of exhaustion, then finally lay still while waiting for my breathing to return to normal.

Suddenly a very clear voice rang out in the room, **"Carolyn, there is no such thing as a punishing God."**

That voice was so distinct and adamant that I actually got to my feet, checked the closet and walked through my apartment to see if I could find its source. Coming up empty, I decided that somehow this disembodied voice had come from inside me! Had my heart spoken out truth once again? Maybe I wasn't so alone on this journey into the unknown. If my misery was *not* God's punishment, then I could no longer look outside myself, nor could I escape to exotic landscapes for the answers I was seeking. So I made a decision. I sat down on my bed, laid my hands on my heart, and I made a deal with "the voice."

"I will commit to doing whatever it takes to recover my health, so I can rebuild my life. All I require is you take care of me financially, and I'll take care of the rest."

My resolve was clear. I had let go of and changed so much, but I was still clinging to the last vestige of the safety net I so carefully constructed for my former life—the J-O-B. Having job-shared for three years, I knew the stress of the classroom was exacerbating my symptoms. When the present school term ended, I would only have one more year until I reached my thirty years of service required for early retirement. However, it was time to let go of it all—to reach out with faith and trust even if it meant cleaning houses until I could retrain for another career. I signed a contract with the district for the entire school year and would honor my commitment, but I would not sign a new contract in the spring.

So my question became: What do I want to be when I grow up? Every profession I thought about did not feel right. There was no passion or excitement around anything I considered, but I kept searching. According to the fifth step of the eightfold path of Buddhism, right livelihood should be enjoyable, profitable, and spiritually healthy work. That sounded perfect, but I needed specifics.

Coming out of meditation one day, it occurred to me that none of the jobs I was considering had appeal because I was going to be creating work no one had ever done before. That meant I must trust that when the time was appropriate, right livelihood utilizing my special skills and talents would fall into place. The other more specific download from that wise part of myself kept urging me to call the district office right away even though it was only late November. I needed to let Al Zamola, the Personnel Director, know I would not be renewing my contract next school year, so a good replacement could be found.

Because I had been so busy traveling and starting the new school term, I was unaware that Al was on a well-deserved sabbatical. Joan Thesius, the Assistant Director, took my call. Joan had been a classroom teacher, then site administrator, and more recently advanced to her a position at the district office. I knew her for years as she worked her way up in the ranks. Not long before, one of her beautiful twin girls had succumbed to breast cancer, and I had been as supportive as possible to her and the family during that time.

"I know I'm only two years short of qualifying for early retirement," I told Joan when I called, "but I can't hang on any longer. My body hurts too much, and I haven't the energy to do right by my students anymore. I just wanted to let you know I will not be renewing my contract in the spring. You will need to find a replacement for me at Silverwood. I'm planning to take a leave of absence and train for some less demanding and stressful type of work."

"Carolyn, you've given twenty-eight years of dedicated service to your students and your community. I want you to apply for disability retirement immediately. Don't wait. Come down and get the necessary papers as soon as you can."

I was stunned. "I gave up on doctors some time ago, Joan. I don't know if I can find a doctor to help with the paper work, but I'll give it a try. I'll come get the forms today—thank you for your kind and reassuring words."

Well, my insurance had changed once again and I was back with Kaiser as my insurance carrier. When I called the appointment desk, ironically I was assigned an oncologist as my primary care physician. I didn't know if that was a good thing or a harbinger of doom, but I kept the appointment. When we met I described my symptoms to my new doctor and all the things I had done to try regaining my health. Then I asked him if he thought that just possibly the stress of duties in the classroom might be exacerbating my symptoms.

"Of course they are" was his immediate answer. "Where's your paper work? I'll fill out the forms and have them ready for you by this afternoon. You can pick them up from the receptionist."

As this incredible angel left the room with my medical disability forms, I just sat on the examining table with tears of gratitude streaming down my face. How could this be happening so fast? I collected the papers at the end of the day and delivered them to the district office. Joan told me my request would now have to be submitted to the school board for approval, but she assured me that would not be a problem. I later discovered that seeing to my disability retirement was one of the last official acts on Joan's part before she left the district. Al was returning to his duties, and Joan was stepping up to fill the position of Dean of Admissions at a nearby university. No wonder she was in such a hurry for me to complete and submit my paper work.

By Valentine's Day, a substitute had been found to finish out my contract for the remainder of the year and my faculty colleagues and I were celebrating my early retirement. I would remain on my current contract until my accumulated sick leave expired the next year. Then my disability compensation would kick in and be approximately the same salary I was making with my job-share situation. And, just in case I missed the fact that "the voice" was holding up its end of the bargain, I was also awarded a sizeable workers' compensation claim. It seems that when a classroom teacher is having health challenges, it is the administrator's responsibility to see what he or she can do to make your classroom duties easier. Two years with the Terrible Five and getting up to snuff with sixth grade curriculum was worth every penny of this extra bit of economic security.

*I call it an Aha! moment.*
*It is the moment when I can hear, when I know,*
*that an answer is being offered to me.*
*All other sounds measurably fade,*
*including the banter in my brain.*
*It's when the answer travels from my heart to my head*
*and says, "This is so."*

*No questions follow, no objections interrupt;*
*Just the recognition that I must listen and follow.*

—*Sharon E. Rainey*

*Sixteen*

# VAGABOND

I walked away from it all: the twenty-five-year marriage, the beautiful suburban home, the mountain cabin and summers in Idaho, and the twenty-eight-year teaching career. It did not take me many weeks to discover I was not cut out to be a house cleaner. I developed great admiration and respect for those who make their living in that way.

In casting about for some way to start producing income, my thoughts went something like this: *If I can make my way across parts of Europe and the South Pacific on my own and thrive in that process, then I can do the same right at home. Here in the Bay Area my biggest expense is housing; if I can reduce or eliminate what I'm paying in rent, my pension will provide me enough disposable income for travel or going back to school.*

With that insight held firmly in mind, I began to network for housesitting opportunities with my faculty friends at Silverwood. When I called one of the sixth grade teachers, Cherie couldn't help me with my request, but she had one of her own.

"Carolyn, I didn't know you were looking for some other means of producing income. Would you consider helping me to decorate my new condo? You're so good at things like that and I have no idea where to begin. I'd be happy to pay you."

Thus, Carolyn's Creative Interiors came into being. Decorating and sewing was more than just a pastime for me. It was an all-consuming passion—a creative escape from the mindless routine of daily survival during my married years. I had fashioned custom slacks and dresses for Cherie in the past, but she always hired a professional interior designer for her home. Recently, she had been through a divorce and was forced to scale down into her much smaller condominium. Now Cherie was reminding me that I had untapped skills and talents that others admired and needed. Since decorating was always so much fun for me, it never crossed my mind that I could actually make money doing it. This was an exciting possibility I had not considered.

When I finished with her condo, Cherie's former sixth grade teaching partner, Mary, presented an even more exciting project for me to consider. Mary raised two children as a single mom on her teacher's salary. About seven years earlier, her now adult daughter had introduced her to a fabulous man. They dated for a few years, then decided to get married. Recently, the love of her life suffered a massive heart attack and died unexpectedly. After they married, the couple had chosen to live in Mary's home in Antioch and rent out his former family home in San Ramon. In order to settle his estate, Mary now faced the overwhelming task of fixing up and disposing of the San Ramon rental in a slow real estate market. Still reeling from grief, Mary asked me if I would be willing to move into the San Ramon house, fix it up, and stage it for resale. She wanted to put it on the market in June when property sales picked up. I could live in the home rent free and she would pay for repairs and upgrades once the house sold. My younger son, Richard, had recently gotten his contractor's license and could help me with the project. It sounded made-to-order, so I gave notice to my landlady and prepared to leave my little apartment for my next step toward a new life.

I really enjoyed the commission, and it was delivered on time and well under budget. The house sold the first week on the market, and I was scrambling to find a new place to call home. Fortunately, I made lasting friends in my Al-Anon support group and one of the ladies invited me to stay in her second bedroom until some other opportunity presented itself. Patricia was an acquaintance of mine when the boys were growing up. Her son, Kevin, and my oldest son, Mike, were close friends all through school. She was an at-home mom through her marriage. Now that the kids were raised and she was divorced from her husband, Patricia had renewed her secretarial skills and acquired a well-paying position with a company in San Francisco's financial district. Her husband hid most of their community property during the dissolution settlement so her little condo was all she salvaged from the first half of her life. Patricia was determined to stay in her current position long enough to qualify for a retirement compensation she could call her own.

I vividly recall a discussion we had one evening. "Carolyn, it seems so strange to me that you left teaching, especially since you were so close to retirement. Here I am scrambling to catch up, and you simply let it all go. I just can't understand why you would do such a thing."

I thought for a moment about an appropriate response. I did not want to go into a lengthy explanation of my physical challenges, so I simply said, "My life is about freedom now, not security. When I selected a career back in the fifties, there were not a lot of careers open to a woman—nurse, teacher, or secretary was about it. Now women have fought for and gained freedoms I never dreamed possible. I want to start exploring possibilities and living new dreams."

Where did that come from? It sounded like another wise insight compliments of my heart.

The next morning I retrieved my phone calls from my voice mail (no such thing as smartphones back in the '80s). One of the messages was from a fascinating man I met a couple of years earlier when I was looking for Mr. Right in all the wrong places. He wanted me to call him right away. I wrote down Harry's phone number and then reflected for a moment on our first encounter. I had initially thought Harry was an attendee at a one of those horrible Thank God It's Friday (TGIF) events designed for singles to mix and mingle. I arrived late to the venue and one glance into the crowded bar revealed the same desperate and tired faces engaged in meaningless conversation while their eyes searched the room for better options. Exhausted at the prospect, I turned and left the bar. On my way out, I noticed a ruggedly handsome man standing alone by the stairs leading up to the second-floor restaurant. His intelligent gaze caught my approach. He straightened then smiled.

Encouraged, I said, "Hello, I'm Carolyn Bourns. You come to these things often?"

He looked a bit puzzled then responded, "Hello to you, Carolyn. I'm Harry, Harry Reich. I come sometimes to this place for dinner."

The voice was the clincher—deep, resonant, and beautifully accented. "You sound like you're from Eastern Europe. Do you mind if I ask from what country?"

"My accent is Romanian," he answered, "but I did not live long there. I grew up in a Russian prison camp until I was seven, then a kibbutz in Israel. I lived in many more countries after that before settling here in the Bay Area."

"It must have been terrible," I commented in a lame attempt to make small talk. "The Russian prison camp, I mean."

"When it is all you know, it's not so bad. My father was a smart man. He knew how to get what my mother and I needed."

As we continued to exchange data, he shared with me that he was waiting for one of his guests to join a group of his friends upstairs for dinner to celebrate the completion of a new and magnificent home he had just built, staged, and put on the market. Did I want to see it? Swept away by his joy and exuberance, I accepted his offer and we exchanged business cards. Then Harry checked his watch and glanced up toward the restaurant.

"I must go," he said apologetically. "My party for dinner will wonder what has happened to me."

He turned and bounded two at a time up the steep staircase. I recall how I flushed with embarrassment, realizing this man had *not* been a part of the evening's singles event, but merely a misplaced dinner host.

When Harry answered my return call, the first thing he said after I asked how he'd been since last we talked was, "Are you sitting down?"

I had placed the call on Patricia's wall phone in the kitchen, so I turned my back to the counter and slid down the face of the cabinet until I was sitting on the cold floor.

"I'm sitting now. What's going on, Harry? Are you all right?"

"Not exactly, Carolyn. I've recently been diagnosed with stage four prostate cancer. It's very aggressive and my PSA count keeps going up very fast. The doctors want to remove my prostate, but that would mean for the rest of my life I would be incontinent and impotent. I'd rather be dead! I'm determined to beat this thing without medical treatment, and I feel I need your help."

I was astonished. I hardly knew this man. He had taken me to lunch once and then we went to see the home he just finished building. At that time he let me know he was in a long-term and loving relationship and his interest in me was strictly platonic.

"What about your partner," I asked. "Can she help you?"

"No. Esther's gone. She left me about six months before my diagnosis. I still don't know why. Between my heart breaking and now this cancer, I can hardly think straight so I'm surrounding myself with healers. My thoughts keep taking me back to our encounter."

He went on to remind me we had discussed the dietary changes I was making to recover my health. Harry was determined he would defeat and cure this scourge ravaging his body, threatening his manhood, his life—doctors be damned.

After I filled him in on my current situation, Harry invited me to move into his spare bedroom. I could help him with a healthy diet, and he could provide me with a place to call home. He gave me his address and asked me to come see the room. Harry's house was located on Colton Boulevard at the top of a very steep hill above the Montclair District in Oakland. Just driving my little Mitsubishi Mighty Max truck up the steep incline to reach Colton was a challenge. I gave up when it came to navigating the precipitous driveway up to his house, so I parked on Colton and used the staircase put in to help visitors access the front door on foot.

By education, Harry was an engineer. About fifteen years previously, he purchased the lot where his house now stood—or should I say, perched. The lot was in a very desirable location, but it was considered by the city to be unbuildable because of its small size and the instability of the soil. All one had to do was tell Harry something was undoable, and he would move heaven and earth to prove you wrong. He engineered a foundation, firmly anchored it to bedrock, and built a three-story structure that seemed suspended out into thin air. Right after he finished construction, the rains came and the ground around the foundation of the house slid down the hill and into the backyard of the residence on Snake Road below his property. Despite this act of nature, the foundation continued to support the structure. It was a marvel of construction and possibilities. Harry continued to procure unbuildable lots for next to nothing and construct bigger and more fantastic homes throughout the Oakland Hills. After my tour of my future home, I knew that if anyone could do it, Harry would prevail over his next challenge.

As expected, the man who climbed mountains all over the world now launched an assault on the cancer raging through his body. He tried every alternative treatment he could get his hands on. I helped as much as I could with the shopping and cooking, but Harry had his own ideas about what was going into his body. I put my foot down on the fermented medicinal mushrooms, however. They smelled just awful, so I relegated the foaming mess downstairs to the unfinished basement. At one point in this process, Harry found a nurse in his neighborhood who was giving him intravenous injections of some contraband medication he had obtained from a chiropractor in Marin County. He encountered a contaminated vial and ended up with a massive blood infection that put him into the Intensive Care Unit (ICU), fighting for his life. He was told to get his affairs in order. Harry was devastated. He had just found and was smitten with a lovely Jewish woman.

"Carolyn, just when it seems things have turned around for me this had to happen." It was devastating to see this once robust and enthusiastic man with tears streaming down his face. "The doctors are not very encouraging about me making it through this infection, I have no living family, and I don't want my estate going to the government. I need your help making out a will. Do you know anyone who could help with that?"

I asked him if he had thought about who his beneficiaries would be, and he gave me four names. He was adamant that he wanted me to execute his will and be one of his beneficiaries. I was very uneasy with this request, but even more uncomfortable turning down the wishes of a dying man. I told him I'd see what I could do. My friend Bob, who was a tax attorney, dusted off his law books and together we researched how to draft a holographic will. I returned to the hospital and helped Harry laboriously write out and sign in his own handwriting what he wanted done with his home and remaining assets in the event of his death. He signed the document and put it into a book on the table by the side of his bed. I went home to a very empty house.

My indestructible housemate was discharged from the hospital six days later with a monitor strapped to his side that dispensed antibiotics automatically night and day for almost a month after his discharge. He recovered fully from the infection, but the metastasis had traveled up his bones and reached his skull by that point. He started experiencing horrible headaches and double vision that made it difficult for him to drive. Reluctantly, he submitted to radiation treatments to lessen his symptoms. I will never forget our conversation the day he received his last radiation treatment.

*Thank God he's back.*

I stood at my bedroom window looking down on the driveway three stories below. Harry's black Trans Am stopped near the foot of the steps leading to the front door. I held my breath as the heavy car door swung open—then nothing.

*I wish I could help him into the house, but he'd hate that.*

Slowly, Harry's dark curls appeared as he shakily pulled himself up to stand next to his low-slung car. Hooking his thumbs into his jeans' pockets, he began the torturous climb up the stairs he had built with his own hands not so many years before. Now this once vigorous man was compelled to rest every third step. Soon, I opened my bedroom door and walked into the enormous living room area. By now Harry had made it as far as the dining room table. He sat staring out at the spectacular three-bridge view of San Francisco Bay. I pulled a chair up next to him and we sat in silence.

"Well, it's done," he said at last. "That was the last radiation treatment. It stopped me seeing two. The pain—it is less, but I'm tired to the inside of my bones."

"That's something I've been wanting to talk to you about," I began.

"Harry, I've been here sharing your beautiful home for over a year—ever since your diagnosis. I've watched you explore every alternative treatment known to man. If there was a cure out there you would have found it. If sheer will, determination, and healthy diet were the answer, you'd be competing right now in a triathlon."

I paused for breath. "And now you're scheduled for your second round of contraband treatment at some neighborhood clinic 500 miles away. You can hardly get up the stairs, for heaven's sake. How do you expect to hop on a plane and go traipsing off to Southern California?"

Harry summoned a reassuring smile. A calm settled about him and he reached to hold my hand.

"My dear Carolyn, I will go back and do the second round of treatments. Not because I believe I'll be made well, but because I must keep going. My search for a cure has become like the mountains I love to climb. If I quit now, it would be like I'm climbing only halfway up."

I sat in stunned silence, marveling at his peaceful tone and the shift that had taken place in Harry's relationship to the disease process raging through his body.

"Harry, say that again."

"Say what?"

"Say what you said just now about the mountains. Just listen—listen to your words. They don't say you're giving up, but they do say you've surrendered. You're finally moving toward a vision of what you want, not running away from or fighting what you fear. There's no sense of protection in your words. Only growth."

He grinned. "Is that what I said?"

"I understand now why you must go, but let me come with you."

"You have your work here, my dear Carolyn," he said, dismissing my offer with a wave of his hand. "I will be fine."

Fine indeed. One short week after Harry left for Orange County, he called. "It's gone!

"What's gone?"

"The cancer. It's gone. My PSA count has dropped to almost normal, and I'm coming home."

"How can that be? You had bone metastasis clear to your skull; your PSA count was above a thousand; you were seeing double and in excruciating pain. Was it the radiation? This second treatment?" A million questions swirled through my head as I tried to grasp what I had just heard.

"They don't think it could be their treatments. It's too soon. And radiation is only to make the symptoms less, not to cure. They don't know what to think."

"Well, I know what to think, Harry. I think you reached the summit! I miss you. The house misses you. Hurry home."

It turned out this was not a fluke, but a genuine spontaneous remission. Because of the radiation treatments Harry was receiving, there were X-rays that showed advanced bone metastasis. When he returned to his doctor about ten days later, not a sign of metastasis could be found, and his PSA count remained almost normal. Harry told me the doctors did not ask about *what* he was doing. The advice was: Whatever you're doing, keep it up.

During my year with Harry, I received some important insights. A new upscale community called Blackhawk had been built at the foot of Mount Diablo. My son was doing some construction work there and had wrangled a couple of interior design commissions for me in the area. I was also helping one of the first grade teachers from Silverwood decorate her new home out in Brentwood. Because I had always been salaried as a public school teacher, I had no idea how to conduct a business. Soon I found I had created a very time-consuming hobby with Carolyn's Creative Interiors, but I was not making any money. The coup de grace was when one of my Blackhawk clients refused to pay me for my work and instead told me I would have to take them to court. This was when I learned how important it was to have a signed contractual agreement—if you wanted to be guaranteed payment at the end of a job. It was obvious to me I needed to learn more about doing business if it was going to be profitable.

My next insight came when I accepted an invitation to attend evening meetings at the same home that had hosted Lin and Stacey Martin for deep-trance channeling. Almost as esoteric, the couple who led these meetings did something called dowsing. Similar to muscle testing and pendulum, dowsing is a way of accessing the subconscious mind for information by asking yes or no questions. The facilitators were Joan (pronounced JoAnne) and Ron Mied, also from Novato. Joan's skill with the dowsing rod was primarily aimed toward helping people with physical and emotional challenges. Using this process, Joan determined that I had a severe magnesium deficiency and recommended products from a company with high-quality herbs and supplements. Soon my bowels relaxed and my symptoms started to ease. That a simple mineral deficiency and my own punishing thoughts about leaving my husband could result in such pain and misery was astonishing to me. I wanted to know more so I could help myself, and possibly others, begin to heal.

At one of the meetings, Joan informed the group that her guidance had let her know she was no longer to dowse answers for others. Instead, from that point on she would be offering classes so we could learn how to communicate with the body and use herbal medicines and supplements independently. She would be teaching a unique constitutional assessment tool called iridology. Constitution can be understood as the reason why three people can abuse their bodies in essentially the same way; one person might develop heart disease, one cancer, and the third might not get sick at all. Knowing a person's constitution helps to determine what body systems in a person are strong or weak. If we can support and strengthen the weak systems with herbs and lifestyle changes and draw from the strong systems, then the body can rebalance and the immune system can fully support true healing. Iris analysis can also help a person to know what supplements to take to maintain health. Thus began my knowledge and passion for natural health.

Now that Harry was well and in love again, it was time for me to move on. The plan was to first visit my family in Washington and then find an apartment when I returned. I had recently received a phone call from my Aunt Care informing me that my cousin Eb had received a diagnosis of colon cancer and had undergone successful surgery to remove the primary tumor, but the cancer had metastasized and spread to his liver.

Growing up, Eb was like a big brother to me—only much nicer than my big brother, Barney. I hoped I could tell him Harry's story and inspire him to keep looking for answers. Eben had graduated from Stanford University with a law degree, following in the footsteps of his father. He was not, however, enthusiastic about his chosen profession and would much rather be out on the golf course, or reading a book on philosophy. He had the most amazing library I have ever seen. Unlike Harry, Eb was a lover, not a fighter, but I thought if he could hear Harry's story it would give him hope, instead of the medical message that he would be dead in three months and needed to get his house in order.

I remember vividly my discussion with Eb in Aunt Care's living room as I tried not to show alarm at the change in this handsome and formerly robust man. I listened quietly as he described his recent journey, then I told him Harry's story. I also remember telling him that the doctor's prediction was coming from the fact that medical treatment has no answers for him, but that did not mean there weren't all kinds of other possibilities. The next thing I told him was that I would be sending him a book and it was important he read it.

In my own search for healing I stumbled upon an amazing book I was sure would help my cousin. The title called to me. *Paradox and Healing: Medicine, Mythology and Transformation* was collaboratively written by two Canadian doctors, Michael Greenwood and Peter Nunn. Transformation was the operative word. On the cover was a picture of a phoenix rising from the ashes. This was a book that combined the science of medicine with the power of myth to inform, transform, and heal. I had experience with transformation and healing, but this added the power of story into the equation. Eb put his house in order, read the book, took my dietary advice, and returned to his doctor eight months later to get the resection and receive the news that he was free of all signs of cancer. Bless his heart. This golf-playing athlete even took up yoga at the urging of his adult children.

*The reason there is a spontaneous remission in any disease*
*is due to quantum body intelligence.*

*It allows the body, without explanations, to heal*
*through any of the activation of specific energy centers*
*the second we have made the shift*
*from fear to love.*

—*Michael Forrester*

*Seventeen*

# FINAL WORDS TO FUTURE GENERATIONS

Thank you, dear ones, for finding time in your busy lives to join me on my journey from the Ordinary World of my childhood to what I now think of as The Paradox of the Other World—that place where transcendence and miracles happen. I liken my experience to the phenomenon of metamorphosis. The lowly caterpillar hatches from eggs and sets about eating everything it can sink its little teeth into until it gets too big for its skin. At that point it spins a very sturdy cocoon around its fuzzy fat body and surrenders to transformation. Inside its cocoon, the caterpillar dissolves into a goo-like substance made up of what scientists call "imaginal cells." In the darkness of this suspended state it will eventually emerge as a magnificent butterfly. Now it is able to regenerate its species into ever more beauteous butterflies. I wonder if letting go of its caterpillarness is as challenging for this creature as it was for me letting go of the Ordinary World?

My big decision to walk away from my teaching career did not mean I was done with education. There are two different Latin roots of the English word 'education.' They are 'educare,' which means *to train* or *to*

*mold* and 'educere,' meaning *to lead out.* The first meaning predominates in our public schools: the preserving and passing down of knowledge and the shaping of youth in the image of their parents and culture.

As a beginning teacher, I recognized that children are naturally curious, so I began to draw upon this natural tendency to help my students simply remember what they already knew. My teaching approach was designed to prepare a new generation for the changes that are to come—to create solutions to problems yet unknown. This approach required my students to think, question, investigate, and create rather than to regurgitate rote memorization of facts and display good study skills. My students always did well on standardized testing even though I never taught to these tests. They learned to think for themselves and figure things out independently by drawing upon experience and research.

Curiosity eventually got the best of me and I decided to return to school myself and see if I could find out more about spontaneous remission. If Harry and cousin Eb could pull off such miraculous healings, then we all must have that capability. In both instances, these men had experienced a change in their relationship to the diagnosis they had received—they gave it new meaning. Instead of waging war against the malignancy raging through their bodies, they embraced it as the great teacher illness can be. By age sixty, I earned an advanced degree in Consciousness Studies at a nearby university. I came away with this one-line definition for that "slippery fish" of science: *Consciousness is the meaning we choose to give our experience.*

The experiences I shared in this memoir showed me how the thoughts, feelings, and emotions programmed by the Ordinary World kept me trapped in a box where I had no choices. The circumstances of my birth and early childhood created a belief system that rendered me blind to my own personal power. I didn't regain my health right away and I didn't do it alone, but all that I learned on my healing journey led me to the eventual service and purpose of my life—my true destiny. My suffering was exactly what I needed to awaken and eventually force me to listen to the message from my heart. Today, at age seventy-eight, I enjoy what I like to refer to as "radiant good health." It is now my honor and privilege to mentor and guide others on their own healing journey.

*You are beginning to understand, aren't you?*
*… the whole world is inside you:*
*In your perspectives and in your heart.*
*That to be able to find peace, you must be at peace within yourself,*
*And to truly enjoy life, you must enjoy who you are.*
*Once you learn how to master this, you will be protected*
*from everything that makes you feel like you cannot go on.*

*The energy you give off based on your beliefs …*
*your emotions … your behavior …*
*the vibrational frequency you give off*
*is what determines the kind of reality experience you have …*
*because physical reality doesn't exist*
*except as a reflection of what you most strongly believe is true for you.*

*That is all that physical reality is.*
*It is literally like a mirror.*

*—Bashar (channeled by Darryl Anka)[1]*

---

*Appendix A*

# THE LIFE YOU WERE BORN TO LIVE

I began this book with a quote from Paulo Coelho's classic little book *The Alchemist: "To realize one's destiny is a person's only obligation."* As I discovered through the events related in Chapter 15, your destiny or life purpose is NOT a J-O-B. When I had the insight to let go of my teaching career and follow a path quite different than the one I inherited from my "tribe," my destiny and purpose found me! I had to change from the inside to help transform the outer Carolyn. I would like to recommend to my young readers a tool that can be helpful in this task.

When I began my journey back in the eighties, it was difficult to access information on self-improvement and self-healing. The library and bookstores were my primary resources. My search uncovered certain authors that provided me with tools to guide the way. In my memoir I mentioned authors such as Louise Hay, Shirley MacLaine, and Gerald Jampolsky. Dan Millman, author of the book *The Way of the Peaceful Warrior*, was also influential. After he experienced a series of miraculous events at a critical time in his life, Dan went on to gather material and publish a body of work that can be extremely beneficial in finding one's destiny. This book is called *The Life You Were Born to Live: A Guide to Finding Your Life Purpose.* Millman uses a combination of astrology and numerology to obtain your unique profile. You can access the book online or at your local bookstore, but the easy way to obtain information pertinent specifically to you is by using the following link: http://www.peacefulwarrior.com/life-purpose-calculator/

Since you now know my story, I think you will be able to see how closely my birthdate calculates to describe my journey. I only wish I'd had access to this tool thirty years ago. See what you think:

27/**9**

2: Balance

7: Trust

**9: Integrity**

All digits have an influence—but the bolded
issue is key to your *hidden calling*.

Those on the 27/9 life path are here to work through issues of balanced responsibility, self-trust, and integrity as they come to trust and follow Spirit manifesting within them and others, living in alignment with the higher wisdom of the heart. Since our life purpose represents an uphill climb, 27/9s eventually confront and have to overcome tendencies to mentalize experience rather than trust their heart. They also need to work through subconscious issues of mistrust and betrayal and open their guarded heart to find and follow the spiritual laws "written" there. In order to access the higher laws of their heart, 27/9s must first let go of their concerns about others' opinions and trust their own higher wisdom revealed in their feelings rather than their mental processes. The 7, however, often leads 27/9s to trust everyone but themselves—teachers, masters, scientific experts, or advisers—and to live by other people's theories. We can all learn from others, but 27/9s in particular are here to place final authority with "the counsel of their heart."

# *Appendix B*

# HEART/BRAIN MEDITATION

Renowned as a pioneer in bringing science, spirituality, and the real world together, best-selling author Gregg Braden is promoting a simple yet profound three-minute meditation technique that has the potential to bring peace to our planet. Working with methods developed by the Institute of HeartMath, Gregg is sharing this tool that, if practiced regularly, can trigger up to 1300 chemical reactions in the body.

The cascade of biochemical reactions initiated through this simple yet profound practice lasts for at least six hours. Some of the beneficial effects include: 1) the release of anti-aging hormones (HGH); 2) improved immune response (SigA); 3) enhanced cardiovascular health; 4) heightened ability to process and recall information quickly; 5) opened channels of communication with our sub-conscious so we can change old beliefs that limit our choices, actions and behaviors; and 6) promoted extraordinary states of deep intuition.

It's quick. It's easy and you will begin to notice results within three days. Go to this link for instruction from Gregg on why and "How to Harmonize the Heart and the Brain:" https://www.youtube.com/watch?v=237WCALmJXQ (12:34), or "HeartMath's Quick Coherence Technique:" https://www.youtube.com/watch?v=8zHuoU8yKLQ (3:54).

# Acknowledgments

Gratitude and appreciation are primal feelings generated by the heart. These feelings result in a corresponding e-motion that helps to set up a resonance between head and heart as described in Appendix B. So, it is with heartfelt gratitude and appreciation that I acknowledge all the dear souls who helped launch me as a first-time published author.

As named and described in my memoir, there were many antagonists, mentors, guides, and teachers (both physical and incarnate) who were instrumental to my transformation. As chaotic as my life was during the last half of the 1980s, I would not have survived without your help to guide my way.

I would like to acknowledge all my past and present clients. I began my health education and consulting practice in 1993. I learned from each of you what I needed to know to better serve those who would follow. It has been my honor and privilege to assist you on your healing journey and witness your courage in that process. Many of you asked me, "When are you going to write your book, Carolyn?" My inadequate reply that nobody reads books any more was simply a poor excuse for my reluctance to put my seat in the chair and write. Thank you for nudging me in this very creative and meaningful direction.

My two amazing sons are next. I am the luckiest mom in the world to have such willing and talented individuals at my beck and call. Mike, my computer genius, without your skills and patience, I would still be struggling to get the manuscript submitted. Richard, without your commitment to help finance this project, *Messages from My Heart* would still be just a collection of memories soon to be forgotten. I so appreciate your loving and generous assistance on my behalf.

A moving and motivating force in my life has been my dear friend

Linda Davis. Linda, you offered your considerable editing skills before I even asked. You have supported me in ways too numerous to count. Your friendship has filled my life to overflowing with joy and adventure. I am so blessed to have you in my life.

Encouragement from friends and acquaintances was considerable. To Betty Arnold: thank you, dear friend, for sharing your writing talent with our book club. By sharing your written accounts of incidents and characters from your past, you inspired me to consider the possibility of writing my own story. I treasure your loyalty and friendship. You were there to lend support during those difficult years so long ago. To this day you continue to check in on me when I turn reclusive. You are also responsible for the gift of being part of your writers' group. I am thrilled to count as support some very lovely and talented women focused on honing their writing skills. I have learned so much from you all: Nancy Fox, Dolly Falvy, Nancy Montoya, and Peggy Shockley. Thank you for your input, encouragement, and editing skills.

Linda Davis, Cheryl Anderson, Aida Cerda, and Kit Porter are my four angels, willing and eager to read my entire manuscript and write a brief endorsement for the back cover. I am honored by and thrilled with your glowing testimonials.

I wish to acknowledge Dr. James Key (a.k.a. James R. Cichoracki, Ph.D.) and his influence with making this book possible. Dr. Key, your amazing instructional skills guided me on the fine points of storytelling, but even more importantly your words of praise gave me the courage to take on this challenging project. I am humbled and ever so grateful for your high praise on my first attempt to publish. You are a great gift to anyone fortunate enough to attend your Story Alchemy Seminars.

Lovely gifts have appeared in my life as I journeyed into becoming a published author. One of the loveliest of these gifts has been finding and working with my editor, Kristen Tate, of The Blue Garret. A lot of changes have taken place grammatically speaking since I learned all the 'rules' to proper English composition. I am especially grateful to Kristen for helping an old dinosaur like me maintain political correctness in my manuscript. Unintentionally, words can wounds when thoughtlessly used. The intent of this book is to give hope and healing, so thank you Kristen for being my great teacher in this respect.

Since this is my first experience with actually publishing something I have written, I wish to acknowledge and thank those behind the scenes at Balboa Press who work so diligently on my behalf to get this book in print and out to the public. Pia Jameson and Jorge Carson, my Check-in Coordinators (CIC), have been extremely patient and kind to this point in the process. I have yet to meet the team awaiting me on this new journey into becoming a published author. Thank you, all.

# About the Author

First time author, Carolyn Bourns is a speaker, thought leader and compelling voice for Health & Wellness. Her ability to deliver astute meanings and emotionally intelligent choices to resolve periods of crisis have put her trainings and consulting services in high demand.

Carolyn entered the health education arena in 1993 after twenty-eight years teaching in the California public schools. Motivated by her own health challenges, and after witnessing a number of miraculous spontaneous remissions, Carolyn returned to academia and earned a master's degree in Consciousness Studies.

In her twenty-plus years of private practice, Carolyn has helped hundreds of individuals sort through emotional factors, hidden core beliefs and complementary therapy options to discover their own capacity to self-heal and achieve radiant vitality and well-being.

Currently Bourns resides in the San Francisco Bay Area close to her two boys and three grandchildren and a great grandchild, baby Hudson.

Printed in the United States
By Bookmasters